MICROWAVE

COOKING

QUICK AND EASY

DI BUSSCHAU

PHOTOGRAPHY BY MIKE ROBINSON

NEW HOLLAND

First published in the UK in 1994 by
New Holland (Publishers) Ltd
37 Connaught Street, London W2 2AZ

ISBN 1 85368 314 0

Editors: Alison Leach and Sandie Vahl
Designer: Petal Palmer
Hand lettering: Andrew van der Merwe
Photographer: Mike Robinson
Stylists: Di Busschau and Helen Lindsey-Clark

Typesetting by Ace Filmsetting Ltd, Frome, Somerset
Reproduction by Unifoto (Pty) Ltd
Printed and bound in Singapore by Tien Wah Press (Pte) Ltd

CONTENTS

INTRODUCTION

People seldom read the instructions at the beginning of the book, so if you are here with me now, you will have the benefit of using these recipes as successfully as I have.

Over the past fifteen years or so, I have seen how microwaves have revolutionized the kitchens of families, single people, chefs and caterers. They are quick, economical to use, compact, easy to keep clean, and ensure a cool and comfortable cooking environment in hot weather. Above all, food cooked in a microwave is healthy food using less fat and providing us with the nutrients and energy we need to cope with the stresses of modern life.

sears and browns the food when it comes into contact with it. Preheat the browning dish according to the manufacturer's instructions. Depending on its size, this will take a maximum of about 8 minutes. Meat should be patted dry, flavoured with herbs or spices and placed immediately in the browning dish. The dish should not be removed from the microwave until cooking is complete as its base must remain very hot to brown the food and therefore it must not make contact with any cool surface. The use of butter, oil or margarine in the browning dish depends on personal preference, but may be omitted.

SERVINGS

All recipes in this book serve four, unless specified otherwise. If *increase* quantities, increase the cooking time proportionally, then *subtract* ⅓ of the total cooking time (for example, 1 baked potato = 4 minutes; 3 baked potatoes = [4 × 3] − 4 = 8 minutes). If you *decrease* quantities, decrease the cooking time proportionally, then *add* ⅓ of the total cooking time (for example, 3 baked potatoes = 8 minutes; 1 baked potato = [8 ÷ 3] + 1⅔ = about 4 minutes).

CONTAINERS

Most types of dishes can be used in the oven, except:
- crockery with silver rims;
- ordinary Tupperware;
- plastic that is not pliable (as with certain plastic jugs);
- metal containers.

For combination ovens, use ovenproof cookware and certain types of plastic-ware that is specially manufactured for use in ovens up to 210°C.

BROWNING DISH

The browning dish, manufactured in various forms, is to the microwave what the frying pan is to the hob. The substance in the base of the dish (mica) absorbs microwave energy, making the base very hot, which then

COOKING ON A RACK

When cooking a dish such as a quiche, where you don't want to end up with a soft, undercooked centre, place the dish on a slightly raised rack. This enables the microwaves to cook from underneath the dish.

COVERING FOOD

Generally, for moist cooking (as with vegetables), the container should be covered securely with a lid or cling film. For dry cooking (as with pies), the food should not be covered.

ORDER OF COOKING

When you are preparing a meal, first cook the food that takes the longest to cook (such as rice and meat) as it will have a longer standing time. Vegetables then can be cooked while the meat is standing.

DEFROSTING

All food should be completely defrosted before cooking in a microwave. It is safer to defrost food quickly in a microwave than to leave it over a long period at room temperature as there is considerably less chance of harmful bacteria building up. Also, important nutrients, flavour and moisture are not lost when food is defrosted quickly. Remember that food should be turned or shielded with small pieces of foil to ensure that it defrosts evenly, and it will continue defrosting while standing.

INGREDIENTS
◆ As the metric and imperial quantities given in every recipe are not interchangeable, follow whichever system of measurement you prefer but do not combine them.
◆ The ingredients are listed in the order in which they are used.
◆ Depending on your personal preference or cholesterol count, butter may be replaced by margarine in all the recipes in this book.
◆ Where cream is used, yoghurt may be substituted — it does not curdle in a microwave.
◆ Fresh herbs and freshly ground spices are best for flavour, but dried herbs and pre-packed spices are more convenient to use. Substitute 5 ml/1 teaspoon dried herbs for 15 ml/1 tablespoon fresh.

COMBINATION OVENS
These ovens use a combination of convection and microwave cooking and have become very popular because the results are impressive. Some combination ovens use convection and microwave energy simultaneously, and other types alternate convection and microwave energy. Much shorter cooking times are required with the former.

A quartz grill is now a feature of most combination ovens and even of some compact microwaves, adding a new dimension to microwave cooking. It can be used independently as well as with either microwave power or convection.

COOKING AND STANDING TIMES
Cooking times vary according to the wattage and make of the microwave. All the cooking times given in the recipes are therefore approximate. These recipes were tested in a 650-watt microwave, so if yours has a higher wattage, it is best to use a shorter cooking time initially and then cook for a little longer if necessary.

Food continues to cook for a short time after being removed from a microwave. This is known as standing time. In those recipes where this is an essential part of the cooking process, it is specified.

RADIATION FACTOR
The risk of exposure to radiation through using a microwave is minimal. Microwaves are electromagnetic waves, similar to those that enable us to watch television. The many safety features include locks and seals that make it impossible to use the microwave if the door is not tightly shut. So just relax and enjoy cooking with your microwave!

MICROWAVE POWER LEVELS

A fundamental difference between microwave and conventional cooking is that control is by time rather than by temperature. Instead of temperature settings as in a conventional oven or adjustable controls on the hob, microwaves have variable power levels that control the speed at which food is cooked.

The terms used to describe the degrees of energy are unfortunately not standardized and can be expressed in words, numerals or, occasionally, as a percentage of the total wattage, by different manufacturers. The following list is merely a guideline:

POWER LEVEL	% POWER
Low	25
Defrost	30
Medium-Low	40
Medium	50
Medium-High	60–70
High	100

There is no exact formula for adjusting cooking times when using microwaves of a different power level to the one specified in a particular cookbook. If the recipes have been tested in a 650-watt microwave, as in this book, and your microwave is, for example, 700 watts, it is suggested you take off 10 seconds for every minute and then check.

Most microwave manufacturers supply detailed instructions for using specific models; they usually also have a cookery advice service staffed by experienced home economists who will be able to tell you what adjustments are needed.

Microwaves are frequently used to heat the ready-prepared recipe dishes that are widely available in supermarkets. Some of these in the UK are now labelled Heating Category A, B and so on to denote the microwave power level, in an attempt to introduce standardized descriptions in the EC.

CHAPTER ONE

Appetizers

APPETIZERS can easily be made at the last minute in the microwave and they can also be prepared in advance and reheated, if necessary, as needed. This tasty selection requires only a simple presentation of crisp lettuce or curly endive leaves and cherry tomatoes.

CHICKEN LIVER PATE

1 small onion, finely chopped
1 clove garlic, crushed
90 g/3 oz butter
3 rashers rindless bacon, chopped
250 g/8 oz chicken livers, cleaned and
   chopped (see Hint, right)
2.5 ml/½ teaspoon dried mixed herbs
salt and freshly ground black pepper to taste
12.5 ml/2½ teaspoons brandy

Microwave the onion, garlic, 30 g/1 oz of the butter and the bacon on High for 4 minutes. Add the livers and mixed herbs and microwave, covered, on High for 4 minutes.

Place in a food processor or blender and blend until smooth. Add the remaining butter, seasoning and brandy. Beat with a wooden spoon until smooth, then press into a serving dish. Refrigerate until ready to serve. (If making a few days in advance, top the pâté with clarified butter — see Hint, page 7.) SERVES 6.

DEVILS ON HORSEBACK

12 prunes, pitted
12 smoked oysters or whole almonds
6 rashers rindless streaky bacon

Soak the prunes in water to cover for 1 hour. Microwave on High for 1½–2 minutes. Drain and cool. Place an oyster or almond inside each prune. Cut the bacon rashers in half and stretch with a knife. Wrap half a rasher around each prune and secure with a cocktail stick. (If preparing in advance, cover with cling film and refrigerate at this stage.) Place in a circle on a dinner plate. Microwave on High for 5–6 minutes. Drain on a paper towel and serve while still warm. SERVES 4–6.

CHICKEN LIVER AND MUSHROOM PATE

155 g/5 oz butter
1 medium onion, finely chopped
1 clove garlic, crushed
250 g/8 oz chicken livers, cleaned and
   chopped (see Hint, below)
10 ml/2 teaspoons finely chopped fresh
   thyme
12.5 ml/2½ teaspoons brandy
155 g/5 oz button mushrooms, sliced
salt and freshly ground black pepper to taste
30 ml/2 tablespoons finely chopped parsley
30 ml/2 tablespoons single cream
6 large black mushrooms, stalks removed
lettuce leaves, tomato wedges and sprigs
   of parsley to garnish

Microwave 45 g/1½ oz of the butter, the onion and garlic on High for 3 minutes. Add the livers and thyme. Cover and microwave on High for 5 minutes, stirring once. Cool slightly, then add the brandy and liquidize. Microwave another 45 g/1½ oz of the butter and the button mushrooms in a bowl on High for 3 minutes. Season, then cool and liquidize. Combine both purées with the parsley and cream. Microwave the remaining butter on High for 40 seconds. Place the mushroom caps on a plate and brush with the melted butter. Cover with a paper towel and microwave on High for 2–3 minutes. Cool. Spoon the pâté into the mushroom caps and place the mushrooms on a bed of lettuce leaves. Garnish with tomato and parsley. SERVES 6.

HINT

If you cook chicken livers whole, pierce the membranes a few times with a skewer to prevent the livers from 'popping' and making a mess in your microwave. As an extra precaution, cover the bowl with pierced cling film.

Devils on Horseback (page 6), Mini Tacos (this page) and Spiced Nuts (this page).

SPICED NUTS

22 g/¾ oz butter
good pinch of garlic salt
5 ml/1 teaspoon garam masala
10–12.5 ml/2–2½ teaspoons curry
    powder
200 g/6½ oz unsalted mixed nuts
2.5 ml/½ teaspoon salt

In a shallow bowl, microwave the butter on High for 40 seconds — until melted. Add the garlic salt, curry powder and mixed nuts. Stir well to coat the nuts. Microwave on High for 4–5 minutes, stirring twice. Cool the nuts on greaseproof paper, then sprinkle them with salt and store in an airtight container. MAKES ABOUT 200 G/6½ OZ.

HINT
To clarify butter, place it in a jug and microwave on Medium-High until boiling (do not burn). Carefully strain off the clear (clarified) butter on top. Use to top pâté, or for frying.

MINI TACOS

The mince mixture can be made in advance and reheated.

5 ml/1 teaspoon oil
1 onion, chopped
2 cloves garlic, crushed
250 g/8 oz lean minced beef
45 g/1½ oz packet bolognaise mix
100 ml/3½ fl oz water
1 large packet rippled potato crisps
strips of tomato and green pepper and
    coarsely grated cheese to garnish

Preheat a browning dish on High for 8 minutes. Add the oil, onion and garlic, and stir well. Microwave on High for 1 minute. Add the mince and stir to break it up. Microwave on High for 3–4 minutes, stirring a few times. Add the bolognaise mix and stir well. Add the water. Microwave on High for 5–6 minutes — until thickened. Place a teaspoonful of the mixture on each crisp and arrange the crisps on a serving plate. Garnish with tomato, green pepper and cheese to give colour, and serve while still warm. SERVES 10.

CHAPTER TWO

Soups

Soups can be made quickly and easily in the microwave and you will find that they have more flavour and better colour than when cooked conventionally. A healthy and versatile selection of vegetable soups, and an inexpensive but tasty fish soup, are given here.

NOTES
- Always use a large casserole — as soup boils over easily — and only half-fill the container.
- Purée soup in a food processor, blender or liquidizer, or push it through a sieve.
- Soups may be cooled down and refrigerated or frozen, covered. Don't add cream or yoghurt before refrigerating or freezing. To serve, defrost, add cream or yoghurt according to recipe, then reheat on Medium–High for a few minutes.

CREAM OF CAULIFLOWER SOUP

1 medium cauliflower, broken into small florets
500 ml/16 fl oz hot chicken stock
45 g/1½ oz butter
45 ml/3 tablespoons plain flour
500 ml/16 fl oz milk
salt and freshly ground black pepper to taste
pinch of freshly grated nutmeg
125 ml/4 fl oz single cream
extra cauliflower florets or crisply fried bacon,
    crumbled, or chopped fresh chives to garnish

In a bowl, microwave the cauliflower and 100 ml/3½ fl oz of the stock, covered, on High for 7 minutes. Drain, reserving the liquid. In a deep bowl, microwave the butter on High for 1 minute. Add the flour and mix well. Gradually stir in the remaining stock, milk and reserved liquid, and stir until smooth. Microwave on High for 5 minutes, stirring twice. Add the cauliflower, seasoning and nutmeg, and microwave on High for about 2 minutes. Stir in the cream, garnish as suggested and serve immediately. Alternatively, process until smooth, stir in the cream and reheat on Medium–High for 2 minutes (do not boil), then garnish and serve.

VARIATION: Use 345 g/11 oz broccoli instead of the cauliflower and garnish with crumbled fried bacon.

CREAMY SPINACH SOUP

This method of pre-cooking spinach and adding it to the soup later will improve the colour of the soup — thus preventing it from becoming a sickly green colour.

500 g/1 lb spinach, shredded and
    washed
45 g/1½ oz butter
1 onion, chopped
25 ml/5 teaspoons plain flour
1 litre/1¾ pints hot chicken stock
5 ml/1 teaspoon lemon juice
salt and freshly ground black pepper to taste
pinch of freshly grated nutmeg
250 ml/8 fl oz single cream or milk

Place the still wet spinach in a casserole and microwave, covered, on High for 3–4 minutes. Set aside. Microwave the butter and onion in a bowl on High for 3 minutes. Stir in the flour, then gradually add the stock. Microwave on High for 6 minutes, stirring a few times. When the mixture has thickened, stir in the lemon juice, seasoning and nutmeg. Add the spinach to the mixture and liquidize. Stir in the cream or milk. Reheat on Medium–High for 2–3 minutes (do not boil) and serve piping hot.

CROUTONS

20 ml/4 teaspoons oil
3 slices bread

Preheat a browning dish on High for 5 minutes. Add the oil. Remove the crusts from the bread and cube the bread. Add the cubes to the browning dish and microwave on High for 1½ minutes. Turn the cubes over and microwave on High for another 1 minute. Drain. Add the croûtons to the soup just before serving.

CARROT VICHYSSOISE

This soup improves with keeping so it may be made a day or two in advance. Although it is traditionally served chilled, it tastes just as good hot.

3 leeks, sliced
1 onion, finely sliced
22 g/¾ oz butter
2 large potatoes, peeled and diced
4 carrots, peeled and sliced
20 ml/4 teaspoons chopped fresh mint
5 ml/1 teaspoon dried oregano
250 ml/8 fl oz hot chicken stock
500 ml/16 fl oz boiling water
salt and freshly ground black pepper to taste
finely grated carrot and a sprig of fresh
    mint to garnish

In a large glass bowl, microwave the leeks and onion in the butter on High for 5–6 minutes — until soft. Add the potatoes, carrots, herbs and chicken stock. Microwave on High for 5 minutes — until boiling. Cover the dish and microwave on Medium-High for about 20 minutes — until the vegetables are soft. Add the boiling water and seasoning; process to a fine purée. Reheat on High until hot or chill in the refrigerator. Garnish with carrot and mint before serving.

CREAMY FISH SOUP

Simple to make and tasty.

2 large onions, finely chopped
40 g/1¼ oz butter
250 g/8 oz hake, cubed
25 ml/5 teaspoons plain flour
750 ml/24 fl oz milk
25 ml/5 teaspoons soured cream
10 ml/2 teaspoons mustard powder
25 ml/5 teaspoons chopped parsley
25 ml/5 teaspoons snipped fresh chives
5 ml/1 teaspoon salt
freshly ground black pepper to taste

Microwave the onions and butter in a large bowl on High for 3–4 minutes. Add the fish and microwave on High for 3 minutes — until cooked. Sprinkle the flour over and stir in. Slowly add the milk, soured cream mixed with the mustard powder, parsley, chives, salt and pepper. Stir well. Microwave on High for about 6 minutes, stirring every 3 minutes — until thickened (do not boil). Serve piping hot.

VARIATION: Make toasted cheese rounds. Place them in soup bowls and pour the soup over them Garnish with paprika and chopped parsley.

Carrot Vichyssoise (this page) and Creamy Spinach Soup (page 8).

Country Vegetable Soup (page 11) and Cream of Pumpkin Soup (page 11).

COUNTRY VEGETABLE SOUP

This is a delicious, thick soup that simply needs a tossed green salad and slices of wholemeal bread or crispy rolls to make a complete meal.

22 g/¾ oz butter
100 g/3½ oz broccoli, broken into small
   florets
100 g/3½ oz potatoes, peeled and diced
100 g/3½ oz onions, chopped
100 g/3½ oz carrots, peeled and grated
45 g/1½ oz red pepper, seeded and diced
45 g/1½ oz turnip, peeled and diced
410 g/13 oz canned chopped tomatoes
salt and freshly ground black pepper to taste
910 ml/29 fl oz hot beef stock

Place the butter, all the vegetables and the seasoning in a large bowl. Cover with pierced cling film and microwave on High for 10–12 minutes, stirring after 5–6 minutes. Stir in the stock, cover and microwave on High for 10–12 minutes — until the vegetables are tender. Taste and adjust seasoning. Purée a third of the mixture in a blender and add to the remaining soup to thicken it, if preferred. Reheat on Medium-High for 1 minute, if necessary, and serve hot.

VARIATIONS: Depending on the season, any combination of vegetables may be selected for this soup.

QUICK WINTER SOUP

Serve this simple soup with thick slices of freshly baked wholemeal bread.

4 leeks, thinly sliced
4 potatoes, peeled and cubed
2–3 carrots, peeled and thinly sliced
2 sticks celery, sliced
30 g/1 oz butter
1 litre/1¾ pints hot chicken stock
salt and freshly ground black pepper to taste

Place all the vegetables in a large casserole with the butter. Microwave on High for 8–10 minutes, stirring a few times. Add half the stock, cover, and microwave on High for 10 minutes. Add the remaining stock and season to taste. Liquidize the soup, reheat on High for 1–2 minutes and serve piping hot.

VARIATIONS: For extra flavour add 45 g/1½ oz soup powder (such as tomato, beef or onion) to the soup after it has been liquidized. Microwave on High for a further 5 minutes.

CREAM OF MUSHROOM SOUP

This soup, garnished with Croûtons (page 8), is perfect to serve as a first course for a dinner party.

250 g/8 oz brown mushrooms, sliced
1 onion, chopped
45 g/1½ oz butter
45 ml/3 tablespoons plain flour
750 ml/24 fl oz hot chicken stock
250 ml/8 fl oz milk
10 ml/2 teaspoons lemon juice
salt and freshly ground black pepper to taste
pinch of freshly grated nutmeg
10 ml/2 teaspoons sherry
12.5 ml/2½ teaspoons chopped parsley
12.5 ml/2½ teaspoons Worcestershire
   sauce
45 ml/3 tablespoons single cream (optional)

Microwave the mushrooms, onion and butter in a large casserole on High for 5–6 minutes. Stir in the flour, then gradually blend in the stock, milk and lemon juice. Cover with pierced cling film and microwave on High for 8 minutes. Add the seasoning, nutmeg, sherry, parsley and Worcestershire sauce. Liquidize the soup if a fine texture is preferred. Reheat on High for 1–2 minutes. Stir in the cream, if using, and serve.

CREAM OF PUMPKIN SOUP

Use leftover pumpkin for a really quick soup.

625 g/1¼ lb cooked pumpkin
625 ml/1 pint hot chicken stock
15 g/½ oz butter
12.5 ml/2½ teaspoons plain flour
10 ml/2 teaspoons soft brown sugar
salt and freshly ground black pepper to taste
pinch of ground ginger
pinch of ground cinnamon
155 ml/¼ pint single cream
extra cream and snipped fresh chives to garnish

Liquidize the pumpkin and stock. Knead together the butter and flour to form a beurre manié and stir it into the pumpkin and stock. Add the sugar, seasoning, spices and cream, and blend in. Pour the mixture into a large bowl. Cover and microwave on Medium-High for 6–8 minutes — until piping hot. Swirl in a little extra cream and sprinkle with chives before serving.

VARIATION: Cooked butternut squash can be substituted for the pumpkin.

CHAPTER THREE

Savoury tarts

SAVOURY TARTS, open pies or quiches make an excellent light meal. They are so easy to put together with a few basic ingredients and are a delicious and versatile way of using up leftovers. Savoury tarts are good served hot or cold and make great picnic fare.

NOTES
- ◆ Puff pastry requires circulating heat to crisp so, when cooked in a microwave, it goes soggy.
- ◆ Shortcrust pastry cooks very well in a microwave, although it does not brown.
- ◆ When making a quiche, tart or a pie with a pastry crust, pre-bake the crust.
- ◆ Always place the pie, tart or quiche on a low rack in the microwave so that the centre will set.

CRUSTLESS SMOKED HADDOCK 'TART'

> 250 g/8 oz smoked haddock, skinned, boned and flaked
> 30 ml/2 tablespoons plain flour
> 3 eggs, beaten
> 1 onion, chopped
> 5 ml/1 teaspoon mustard powder
> 12.5 ml/2½ teaspoons chopped parsley
> 100 g/3½ oz Cheddar cheese, grated
> 250 ml/8 fl oz milk
> paprika to taste

Mix the flaked haddock, flour, eggs, onion, mustard powder and parsley together. Stir in the cheese, then mix in the milk. Pour the mixture into a pie dish and sprinkle with paprika. Microwave on Medium for 12–14 minutes — until the tart sets in the middle. Stand for about 5 minutes before serving.

COMBINATION OVEN: Cook at 200 °C temperature and medium-low microwave power level for 12–14 minutes (20–25 minutes if your oven alternates convection and microwave energy).

VARIATIONS: Use smoked trout or mackerel or a mixture of seafood instead of the haddock.

SAVOURY VEGETABLE TART

A delicious and easy-to-make tart that forms its own base.

> 250 g/8 oz courgettes, grated or sliced
> 155 g/5 oz tomatoes, peeled and chopped (see Hint, page 17)
> 1 medium onion, chopped
> 100 g/3½ oz mushrooms, sliced
> 25 ml/5 teaspoons chopped parsley
> 375 ml/12 fl oz milk
> 60 g/2 oz plain or wholemeal flour
> 5 ml/1 teaspoon salt
> pinch of freshly ground black pepper
> pinch of cayenne pepper
> 5 ml/1 teaspoon dried mixed herbs
> 3 eggs
> 100 g/3½ oz Cheddar cheese, grated
> 25 ml/5 teaspoons dried breadcrumbs, seasoned
> paprika to taste

Layer the courgettes, tomatoes, onion, mushrooms and parsley in a deep, greased pie dish. Beat the milk, flour, salt, black pepper, cayenne pepper, herbs and eggs together until smooth. Pour the mixture over the vegetables. Sprinkle the cheese and then the breadcrumbs on top. Dust with paprika. Microwave on Medium-High for 14–15 minutes — until the centre is set. Stand for about 5 minutes before serving.

COMBINATION OVEN: Cook at 200 °C temperature and medium-low microwave power level for 12–14 minutes (16–20 minutes if your oven alternates convection and microwave energy).

VARIATIONS: To make this a meaty dish, use 200 g/6½ oz cooked and chopped chicken, or diced ham, or 200 g/6½ oz canned corned beef or 200 g/6½ oz canned tuna, drained and flaked, instead of the mushrooms and courgettes.

ASPARAGUS QUICHE

BASE
125 g/4 oz self-raising flour
salt to taste
freshly ground black pepper to taste
dried mixed herbs to taste
75 g/2½ oz butter or margarine
1 egg, beaten

FILLING
440 g/14 oz canned asparagus cuts, drained
3 eggs, beaten
200 ml/6½ fl oz milk
5 ml/1 teaspoon dried mixed herbs
25 ml/5 teaspoons plain flour
salt to taste
freshly ground black pepper to taste
freshly grated nutmeg to taste
155 g/5 oz hard cheese of your choice, grated
paprika to taste

To make the base, combine the flour, seasoning and herbs. Rub in the butter or margarine. Add the egg and mix well to obtain a smooth, pliable dough. Roll out the dough thinly and use to line a pie dish. Prick the dough with a fork, cover the dish with a paper towel and microwave on High for 2–3 minutes.

Spread the asparagus cuts over the cooked pastry base. Combine the remaining ingredients for the filling, except the cheese and paprika, and beat well. Pour the mixture over the asparagus. Sprinkle with cheese and paprika. Microwave on Medium-High for 14–15 minutes. Stand for 5 minutes before serving.

VARIATIONS
Instead of the asparagus cuts, use:
◆ 315 g/10 oz mushrooms, sliced, 4 rashers bacon, chopped and 1 onion, finely chopped. Microwave in a bowl on High for 3–4 minutes.
◆ 200 g/6½ oz canned tuna, drained, sliced tomato and chopped fresh herbs.
◆ 200 g/6½ oz leftover chicken, cold meats or vegetables.

Instead of the 200 ml/6½ fl oz milk, use:
◆ 100 ml/3½ fl oz milk and 100 ml/3½ fl oz single cream.
◆ 200 ml/6½ fl oz plain yoghurt.
◆ 170 g/5½ oz canned evaporated milk.

Instead of the pastry base, use:
◆ 200 g/6½ oz cheese-flavoured biscuits, crushed, combined with 75 g/3½ oz butter or margarine, melted.

Savoury Vegetable Tart (page 12).

CHAPTER FOUR

Pasta

PASTA has become everyone's favourite food, as it is not only a great source of energy but it is also very versatile. Like rice and other grains, pasta does not cook faster in a microwave. However, it won't stick to the dish, burn or steam up the kitchen.

PASTA NEAPOLITAN

200 g/6½ oz spaghetti
785 ml/1¼ pints boiling water
5 ml/1 teaspoon salt
5 ml/1 teaspoon oil
10 g/¼ oz butter

NEAPOLITAN SAUCE
625 g/1¼ lb tomatoes, peeled and
    quartered (see Hint, page 17)
1 clove garlic, crushed
25 ml/5 teaspoons tomato paste
12.5 ml/2½ teaspoons soft brown sugar
2.5 ml/½ teaspoon salt
5 ml/1 teaspoon dried basil
12.5 ml/2½ teaspoons chopped parsley
12.5 ml/2½ teaspoons cornflour
15 ml/1 tablespoon water

60 ml/4 tablespoons grated Parmesan or
    Cheddar cheese
chopped parsley and black olives to garnish

Microwave the pasta, water, salt and oil in a large glass or plastic bowl, uncovered, on High for 8 minutes, stirring after 4 minutes. Stand for 5 minutes, then drain and toss in the butter.

To make the sauce, place the tomatoes, garlic and tomato paste in a food processor, blend until smooth and pour into a glass bowl. Add the sugar, salt, basil and parsley. Blend the cornflour and water to a paste and add, stirring well. Microwave on High for 6–8 minutes, stirring after 3 minutes. Stand for 2–3 minutes. While the sauce is standing, reheat the pasta on High for 1–2 minutes. Pour the sauce over the pasta, sprinkle with cheese and parsley, dot with olives and serve.

VARIATIONS: You can add 100 g/3½ oz chopped mushrooms or ham, mussels, shrimps or clams to the sauce.

BAKED MACARONI AND CHICKEN

200 g/6½ oz macaroni
1 litre/1¾ pints boiling water
5 ml/1 teaspoon salt
5 ml/1 teaspoon oil
1 onion, chopped
1 stick celery, chopped
22 g/¾ oz butter
100 g/3½ oz mushrooms, sliced
200 g/6½ oz tomatoes, peeled and
    chopped (see Hint, page 17)
2.5 ml/½ teaspoon dried basil
salt and freshly ground black pepper to taste
315 g/10 oz chicken breasts, skinned,
    boned and cubed
1 egg
250 ml/8 fl oz low-fat plain yoghurt
75 g/2½ oz Cheddar cheese, grated
paprika to taste

Break the macaroni into pieces and place it in a large bowl with the water, salt and oil. Microwave, uncovered, on High for 10–12 minutes, stirring after 6 minutes. Stand for 5 minutes, then drain.

Microwave the onion, celery and butter in a bowl on High for 3 minutes. Add the mushrooms, tomatoes, basil, seasoning and chicken. Cover and microwave on High for 3–4 minutes, stirring once.

Add the macaroni to the chicken mixture and spoon into a casserole. Beat the egg and yoghurt together until smooth; stir in the cheese. Pour the mixture over the macaroni and chicken, sprinkle with paprika, and microwave on Medium-High for 12–14 minutes. Stand for about 4 minutes, then serve.

COMBINATION OVEN: Cook at 200 °C temperature and medium-low microwave power level for 12–14 minutes (20–25 minutes if your oven alternates convection and microwave energy).

Pasta Neapolitan (page 14) and Spinach and Pasta Bake (page 17).

TAGLIATELLE WITH CREAMY HAM SAUCE

This is really quick to make and delicious with a tossed green salad and crispy French bread.

250 g/8 oz tagliatelle
1 litre/1¾ pints boiling water
5 ml/1 teaspoon salt
5 ml/1 teaspoon oil

CREAMY HAM SAUCE
22 g/¾ oz unsalted butter
125 ml/4 fl oz double cream
45 g/1½ oz Parmesan cheese, grated
60 g/2 oz ham, cubed

freshly ground black pepper to taste
chopped parsley to garnish

Place the pasta, water, salt and oil in a large bowl and microwave, uncovered, on High for 6–8 minutes, stirring after 3 minutes. Stand for 5 minutes, then drain.

To make the sauce, microwave the butter in a bowl on High for 50 seconds — until melted. Mix the cream and half the cheese in well. Add the ham.

Mix the tagliatelle with the sauce and add pepper. Reheat gently on Medium for 1–2 minutes. Sprinkle with the remaining cheese, garnish with parsley and serve.

PASTA WITH PEPPERS

1 onion, finely chopped
2 cloves garlic, crushed
1 red and 1 yellow pepper, seeded and
    cut in julienne strips
100 ml/3½ fl oz tomato paste
45 ml/3 tablespoons dry white wine
salt and freshly ground black pepper to taste
25 ml/5 teaspoons chopped fresh basil
100 g/3½ oz olives, pitted
250 g/8 oz fusilli or penne
1 litre/1¾ pints boiling water
5 ml/1 teaspoon salt
5 ml/1 teaspoon oil
100 g/3½ oz feta cheese, crumbled

Microwave the onion, garlic and peppers in a large bowl on High for 5–6 minutes — until the vegetables soften slightly. Add the tomato paste and wine and microwave on High for 6 minutes. Season, add the basil and olives then microwave on High for 3 minutes. Cover and keep warm while cooking the pasta.

Microwave the pasta, water, salt and oil in a large bowl on High for 8–10 minutes, stirring after 4 minutes — until cooked. Stand for 5 minutes, then drain.

Pour the pepper sauce over the pasta and sprinkle with feta cheese to serve.

Tagliatelle with Creamy Ham Sauce (this page) and Pasta with Peppers (this page).

SPINACH AND PASTA BAKE

A tasty dish that is perfect for vegetarians.

250 g/8 oz penne
1 litre/1¾ pints boiling water
5 ml/1 teaspoon salt
5 ml/1 teaspoon oil
250 g/8 oz frozen creamed spinach,
    thawed and drained
pinch of freshly grated nutmeg
3 eggs, beaten
410 g/13 oz canned cream of mushroom soup
90 g/3 oz Cheddar cheese, grated
salt and freshly ground black pepper to taste
paprika to taste

Place the pasta, water, salt and oil in a large bowl and microwave, uncovered, on High for 8–10 minutes, stirring after 4 minutes. Stand for 5 minutes, then drain and place in a deep casserole.

Spoon the spinach over the pasta and sprinkle with nutmeg. Mix the eggs with the soup and pour over the spinach, then sprinkle with cheese, seasoning and paprika. Microwave on Medium-High for 8–10 minutes — until firm. Stand for 2–3 minutes, then serve.

COMBINATION OVEN: Cook at 200 °C temperature and medium-low microwave power level for 12–14 minutes (20–25 minutes if your oven alternates convection and microwave energy).

TUNA AND PASTA BAKE

185 g/6 oz pasta shells or fusilli
1 litre/1¾ pints boiling water
5 ml/1 teaspoon salt
5 ml/1 teaspoon oil
200 g/6½ oz canned tuna, drained
440 g/14 oz canned tomatoes, drained
    and chopped
200 g/6½ oz button mushrooms, sliced
10 ml/2 teaspoons lemon juice
dash of Tabasco sauce
25 ml/5 teaspoons chopped parsley
salt and freshly ground black pepper to taste
5 ml/1 teaspoon dried oregano

TOPPING
315 ml/½ pint plain yoghurt
1 egg
60 g/2 oz plain flour
5 ml/1 teaspoon mustard powder
75 g/2½ oz Cheddar cheese, grated

Place the pasta, water, salt and oil in a large bowl and microwave, uncovered, on High for 8–10 minutes, stirring after 4 minutes. Stand for 5 minutes, then drain and place in a casserole. Break up the tuna and stir into the pasta with the tomatoes, mushrooms, lemon juice, Tabasco, parsley, seasoning and oregano.

To make the topping, blend the yoghurt and egg. Gradually add the flour, mustard, seasoning and cheese. Pour over the pasta mixture and microwave on Medium-High for 12–15 minutes — until the topping is set. Stand for 4–5 minutes, then serve.

COMBINATION OVEN: Cook on 200 °C temperature and medium-low microwave power level for 12–14 minutes (20–25 minutes if your oven alternates convection and microwave energy).

HINT
To peel tomatoes easily, wash the tomatoes (but don't dry), then microwave on High for 20–30 seconds per tomato. Peel immediately.

CURRIED PASTA SALAD

Simple to make as a light lunch in summer.

250 g/8 oz elbow macaroni
1 litre/1¾ pints boiling water
5 ml/1 teaspoon salt
5 ml/1 teaspoon oil
12.5 ml/2½ teaspoons butter
1 onion, chopped
1 green pepper, seeded and diced
15 ml/1 tablespoon curry powder
1 pineapple, peeled and cubed
125 ml/4 fl oz mayonnaise
25 ml/5 teaspoons chutney
chopped parsley or chives to garnish

Place the macaroni, water, salt and oil in a large plastic or glass bowl and microwave, uncovered, on High for 10–12 minutes, stirring after 5 minutes. Stand for 5 minutes, then drain.

In a glass bowl, microwave the butter, onion and green pepper on High for 3 minutes. Drain and cool. Mix together the curry powder, pineapple, mayonnaise and chutney, then mix with the onion and green peppers. Mix in the macaroni. Refrigerate until ready to serve. Garnish with parsley or chives.

VARIATIONS: Use 2–3 chopped peaches or apricots or sliced bananas instead of the pineapple.

CHAPTER FIVE

Seafood

SEAFOOD, whether baked in a sauce or 'fried' in the browning dish, cooks very quickly in a microwave and retains its superbly delicate flavour and texture. An interesting variety of tastes is catered for in this selection of easy-to-prepare dishes.

NOTES

◆ Seafood is best cooked fresh but frozen is sometimes the only option. Defrost completely before cooking.
◆ Arrange fish fillets with the thin parts to the centre or they will overcook.
◆ Test if fish is cooked by inserting a knife into the thickest part of the flesh — it should be opaque and should flake easily. The flesh of shellfish will turn opaque when cooked and the shells will turn pink.

CRUMBED SOLES

Serve these delicious 'fried' soles with Creamed Spinach (page 36) or Carrots with Soured Cream (page 37) and New Potatoes (page 40).

> 75 g/2½ oz plain flour
> pinch of salt
> pinch of lemon pepper
> 4 dressed lemon soles
> 1 egg, lightly beaten
> 125 g/4 oz dried breadcrumbs,
>   seasoned
> 100 ml/3½ fl oz oil
> 1 lemon, cut into wedges

Mix the flour with the salt and lemon pepper. Dip the soles into the flour, then into the egg, then coat with the breadcrumbs. Refrigerate for 30 minutes to prevent the crumb mixture from coming away from the fish during cooking.

Preheat a browning dish on High for 8 minutes. Add the oil and microwave on High for 1 minute. Place the soles in the dish and microwave on High for 2 minutes. Turn over and microwave on High for another 2–3 minutes. Drain, then arrange on a serving platter with the lemon wedges.

BAKED LEMON FISH FILLETS WITH CREAMY SAUCE

New potatoes and a crisp green salad make perfect accompaniments to this dish.

> 15 ml/1 tablespoon butter
> 15 ml/1 tablespoon lemon juice
> 750 g/1½ lb fish fillets (such as hake,
>   cod, plaice or haddock)
> 2.5 ml/½ teaspoon dried dill or parsley
> pinch of pepper

> CREAMY SAUCE
> 22 g/¾ oz butter
> 25 ml/5 teaspoons plain flour
> 250 ml/8 fl oz hot fish stock (add milk to
>   reserved cooking juices to make up
>   quantity)
> pinch of cayenne pepper
> 5 ml/1 teaspoon grated lemon zest
> salt to taste

Microwave the 15 ml/1 tablespoon butter in a bowl on High for 20 seconds to melt, mix with the lemon juice and pour over the fish. Sprinkle with dill or parsley and pepper. Microwave on High for 7½ minutes (1 minute per 100 g/3½ oz fish). Drain and reserve the cooking juices. Keep the fish warm.

To make the sauce, microwave the butter in a bowl on High for 20 seconds to melt, mix in the flour, then stir in the stock. Microwave on High for 3–4 minutes, stirring after 2 minutes — until thickened. Add the cayenne pepper, lemon zest and salt. Pour the hot sauce over the fish to serve.

VARIATIONS
◆ Add 100 g/3½ oz peeled prawns to the sauce.
◆ Add 2.5–5 ml/½–1 teaspoon curry powder to the flour.

Baked Lemon Fish Fillets with Creamy Sauce (page 18) and Creamy Baked Mustard Fish (page 20).

BAKED FISH IN MUSHROOM SAUCE

750 g/1½ lb fish fillets
410 g/13 oz canned mushroom soup
25 ml/5 teaspoons milk
30 ml/2 tablespoons sherry
pinch of cayenne pepper
salt to taste
100 g/3½ oz Cheddar cheese, grated

Pat the fish dry and layer it in a shallow dish.

Place the soup in a jug and microwave on High for 3 minutes. Stir in the milk, sherry, cayenne pepper and salt, and pour over the fish. Sprinkle the cheese on top. Microwave on High for 10½–11 minutes (1 minute per 100 g/3½ oz fish plus 3–4 minutes for the sauce). Stand for 3–4 minutes before serving.

TUNA FISH BAKE

Serve this very simple dish with Savoury Rice (page 39) and a crisp green salad.

410 g/13 oz canned tuna, drained and flaked
100 g/3½ oz pasta (such as elbow macaroni), cooked
410 g/13 oz canned cream of mushroom soup
2 eggs, beaten
12.5 ml/2½ teaspoons chopped parsley
salt and freshly ground black pepper to taste

Mix all the ingredients together thoroughly, then spoon into a deep, round soufflé dish. Smooth the top. Microwave on Medium-High for 12–14 minutes — until the mixture is firm and cooked through. Stand for about 4 minutes, then serve as suggested.

FISH LOAF WITH TOMATO MAYONNAISE

500 g/1 lb fish fillets
dash of lemon juice
salt and freshly ground black pepper to taste
200 g/6½ oz canned salmon, drained
1 onion, finely chopped
15 g/½ oz butter
45 ml/3 tablespoons chopped gherkins
1 slice pimiento, diced
5 ml/1 teaspoon salt
pinch of freshly ground black pepper
25 ml/5 teaspoons lemon juice
3 eggs, separated
45 g/1½ oz butter
45 ml/3 tablespoons plain flour
250 ml/8 fl oz hot fish stock (add milk to reserved
    cooking juices to make up quantity)

TOMATO MAYONNAISE
3 ripe tomatoes, peeled and chopped (see
    Hint, page 17)
salt and freshly ground black pepper to taste
pinch of caster sugar
pinch of dried dill
45 ml/3 tablespoons tomato paste
1 clove garlic, crushed
155 ml/¼ pint mayonnaise

Sprinkle the fish fillets with the lemon juice and season-ing, and microwave, covered, on High for 5 minutes (1 minute per 100 g/3½ oz fish). Cool and drain, reserving the cooking juices. Blend the fish fillets and salmon together in a food processor. Microwave the onion and 15 g/½ oz butter in a bowl on High for 3 minutes. Mix in the fish mixture, gherkins, pimiento, salt, pepper, lemon juice and egg yolks.

Microwave the 45 g/1½ oz butter on High for 40 seconds to melt. Stir in the flour; slowly add the stock. Microwave on High for 2 minutes, stir, then microwave on High for 1–2 minutes — until the sauce thickens. Mix the sauce into the fish mixture. Beat the egg whites until stiff and fold into the mixture. Spoon into a greased 1-kg/ 2-lb loaf pan. Microwave on Medium-High for 12–14 minutes — until firm and set. Keep warm.

To make the tomato mayonnaise, mix together the tomatoes, seasoning, sugar, dill, tomato paste and garlic. Microwave on High for 4 minutes. Cool, push through a sieve, then stir in the mayonnaise.

Turn out the fish loaf and serve it sliced with the tomato mayonnaise.

COMBINATION OVEN: Cook on 200 °C temperature and medium-low microwave power level for 15 minutes (20 minutes if your oven alternates convection and micro-wave energy).

KING PRAWNS WITH LEMON AND GARLIC SAUCE

Eating out is so expensive, so why not try something special at home? Serve these delicious king prawns on a bed of Savoury Rice (page 39), with a green salad on the side and some crusty bread.

16 large king prawns, cut in half

LEMON AND GARLIC SAUCE
100 g/3½ oz butter
10 ml/2 teaspoons lemon juice
2 cloves garlic, crushed
12.5 ml/2½ teaspoons chopped parsley

Place the king prawns in a flat-bottomed dish. Cover with pierced cling film and microwave on High for 3–4 minutes, stirring after 2 minutes. Arrange the prawns on a serving dish and cover to keep warm while you make the lemon and garlic sauce.

Place the butter, lemon juice and garlic in a bowl and microwave on High for 2–3 minutes. Stir in the parsley and pour the sauce into a serving jug.

CREAMY BAKED MUSTARD FISH

This is a very colourful dish and it tastes delicious!

750 g/1½ lb firm fish fillets (such as cod,
    haddock or hake)
1 onion, chopped
½ red pepper, seeded and diced
1 clove garlic, crushed
200 g/6½ oz button mushrooms, sliced
salt and freshly ground black pepper to taste
2.5 ml/½ teaspoon dried dill
200 ml/6½ fl oz soured cream
5 ml/1 teaspoon Dijon mustard
pinch of caster sugar
paprika to taste

Dry the fish fillets with a paper towel and arrange them in a shallow dish.

Combine the onion, red pepper, garlic and mush-rooms in a small bowl, cover and microwave on High for 4–5 minutes. Spread the mixture over the fish fillets. Season and sprinkle with dill. Mix together the soured cream, mustard and sugar and pour the mixture over the fish. Sprinkle with paprika. Microwave on High for about 10 minutes (1 minute per 100 g/3½ oz fish plus 3–4 minutes for the sauce). Stand for about 3 minutes, then serve with spinach and mashed potatoes.

HONEY SPICED FISH

Serve this gently curried fish with a bowl of rice.

750 g/1½ lb fish fillets (such as plaice or
    lemon sole)
12.5 ml/2½ teaspoons Dijon mustard
15 ml/1 tablespoon clear honey
10 ml/2 teaspoons lemon juice
pinch of curry powder
paprika to taste
chopped parsley to garnish

Place the fish in a casserole. Mix the remaining ingredients together in a jug, except the paprika and parsley, and microwave on High for 20 seconds. Pour over the fish. Dust with paprika. Microwave on High for 8 minutes (about 1 minute per 100 g/3½ oz fish). Stand for 2 minutes, garnish with parsley and serve.

VARIATION: Place the fish under a preheated grill for 2 minutes before serving.

QUICK JAMBALAYA

Add fresh crusty rolls for a quick meal.

30 g/1 oz butter
1 onion, chopped
1 green pepper, seeded and chopped
2 cloves garlic, crushed
200 g/6½ long-grain white rice
410 ml/13 fl oz hot fish or chicken stock
410 g/13 oz canned chopped tomatoes
100 g/3½ oz button mushrooms, sliced
salt and freshly ground black pepper to taste
dash of Tabasco sauce
200 g/6½ canned tuna or mussels,
    drained, or 200 g/6½ oz cooked and
    chopped chicken

Microwave the butter, onion, green pepper and garlic in a bowl on High for about 5 minutes. Mix in the remaining ingredients. Cover and microwave on High for about 20 minutes. Stand for 10 minutes, fluff with a fork and serve.

Fish Loaf with Tomato Mayonnaise (page 20) and Quick Jambalaya (this page).

Haddock Kedgeree (page 23) and Curried Fish Fillets (page 23).

FISH IN ASPARAGUS SAUCE

750 g/1½ lb fish fillets
410 g/13 oz canned cream of asparagus
   soup
125 ml/4 fl oz dry white wine
5 ml/1 teaspoon dried basil
1 bayleaf

Pat the fish fillets dry and layer them in a shallow dish. Mix together the soup, wine and herbs. Pour the mixture over the fish. Microwave on High for 10½–11 minutes (1 minute per 100 g/3½ oz fish plus 3–4 minutes for the sauce). Stand for 3–4 minutes, remove the bayleaf, then serve with a green salad.

PAN-FRIED TROUT WITH MUSHROOM AND GARLIC SAUCE

The creamy sauce is a real treat.

45 ml/3 tablespoons plain flour
salt and freshly ground black pepper to taste
4 trout, cleaned
30 g/1 oz butter

MUSHROOM AND GARLIC SAUCE
250 g/8 oz button mushrooms, sliced
1 clove garlic, crushed
45 ml/3 tablespoons dry white wine
125 ml/4 fl oz double cream
salt and freshly ground black pepper to taste

Mix the flour and seasoning together. Pat the fish dry and coat it in the seasoned flour. Preheat a browning dish on High for 8 minutes. Add the butter, then the trout and microwave on High for 2 minutes. Turn the trout over and microwave on High for another 5½ minutes. Remove the trout, drain on a paper towel and cover to keep warm while making the sauce.

To make the sauce, add the mushrooms and garlic to the butter in the browning dish. Microwave on High for 3–4 minutes. Add the wine and microwave on High for 1 minute. Stir in the cream and microwave on High for 1 minute. Season. Arrange the trout in a serving dish, pour the sauce over and serve.

NOTE: If cooking a whole fish, remove the eyes (or ask your fishmonger to do so!) or they tend to 'pop' out.

VARIATION: Scatter toasted almonds over the sauce-covered trout. To toast almonds, spread them over the base of a preheated browning dish and microwave on High for 4–5 minutes, stirring every minute.

CURRIED FISH FILLETS

750 g/1½ lb firm fish fillets (such as cod)

CURRY SAUCE
30 g/1 oz butter
5 ml/1 teaspoon grated fresh ginger
1 onion, chopped
½ red chilli, seeded and chopped
4 spring onions, chopped
1 clove garlic, crushed
5–10 ml/1–2 teaspoons curry powder
45 ml/3 tablespoons water
75 ml/2½ fl oz dry sherry or white wine
10 ml/2 teaspoons cornflour
salt to taste

Pat the fish dry and layer it in a shallow dish.

To make the sauce, microwave the butter, ginger, onion, chilli, spring onions, garlic and curry powder in a glass bowl on High for 3–4 minutes. Mix together the water, sherry or wine, cornflour and salt, and add to the bowl. Pour the sauce over the fish, then microwave on High for 8–10 minutes (1 minute per 100 g/3½ oz fish plus 3–4 minutes for the sauce). Stand for 3 minutes, then serve.

HADDOCK KEDGEREE

You will need to boil eggs on the hob for this dish.

250 ml/8 fl oz milk
500 g/1 lb smoked haddock or cod
1 onion, chopped
½ green or red pepper, seeded and diced
1 stick celery, chopped
200 g/6½ oz button mushrooms, sliced
45 g/1½ oz butter
3 hard-boiled eggs, chopped
30 ml/2 tablespoons chopped parsley
2.5 ml/½ teaspoon dried thyme
salt and freshly ground black pepper to taste
375 g/12 oz cooked rice (see page 39)
1 hard-boiled egg, quartered, or chopped
   parsley or sprig of fresh thyme to garnish

Pour the milk over the fish and microwave on High for about 6 minutes. Drain the fish, remove the skin and flake the flesh coarsely, removing any bones. Microwave the onion, green pepper, celery, mushrooms and butter on High for 5–6 minutes, stirring after 2–3 minutes. Mix in the fish, then the eggs, herbs, seasoning and rice. Microwave on High for 4 minutes. Garnish with egg, parsley or thyme to serve.

Chicken

CHICKEN cooks much more quickly in a microwave than it does when cooked using conventional methods and the results are tender and juicy. A wide range of tastes and occasions is catered for in this appetizing selection of simple-to-make dishes.

NOTES
◆ The skin of the chicken does not brown or crisp when cooked in a microwave, so you will have to make use of browning agents or the browning dish.
◆ For even cooking, arrange chicken portions so that the thicker parts are towards the outer edge of the dish.

STUFFED ROAST CHICKEN

STUFFING
1 stick celery, finely chopped
1 onion, finely chopped
10 ml/2 teaspoons butter
5 ml/1 teaspoon dried mixed herbs
salt and freshly ground black pepper to taste
60 g/2 oz pecan nuts, chopped
1 egg, lightly beaten
90 g/3 oz fresh breadcrumbs

1 chicken
15 ml/1 tablespoon butter, melted
    (optional)
2.5 ml/½ teaspoon paprika

To make the stuffing, microwave the celery, onion and butter in a bowl on High for 3–4 minutes. Stir in the herbs, seasoning, nuts and egg, then the breadcrumbs.

Clean the chicken, fill the cavity with the stuffing, truss and weigh. Brush with melted butter, if using, then sprinkle with the spices. Preheat a browning dish on High for 8 minutes. Place the chicken, breast-side down, in the dish. Microwave on High for 1 minute, turn over on to the other breast and microwave on High for 1 minute, turn again and microwave on High for 3 minutes. Cover the chicken with a hood of waxed paper, then microwave on Medium-High for 10 minutes per 500 g/1 lb. Stand for about 10 minutes, carve and serve.

COMBINATION OVEN: Cook at 230 °C temperature and medium microwave power level for 10 minutes per 500 g/1 lb (12–14 minutes if your oven alternates convection and microwave energy).

CHICKEN DRUMSTICKS WITH BARBECUE MARINADE SAUCE

Serve these deliciously tangy chicken drumsticks hot or cold with salads of your choice. They make wonderful picnic fare accompanied by a rice salad.

750 g/1½ lb chicken drumsticks

BARBECUE MARINADE SAUCE
125 ml/4 fl oz tomato ketchup
75 ml/2½ fl oz chutney
2.5 ml/½ teaspoon Tabasco
25 ml/5 teaspoons Worcestershire sauce
25 ml/5 teaspoons soy sauce
45 ml/3 tablespoons red wine
5 ml/1 teaspoon garlic powder
5 ml/1 teaspoon salt
5 ml/1 teaspoon freshly ground black pepper
5 ml/1 teaspoon paprika

Place the chicken drumsticks in a large round dish, thick parts towards the outside. Mix all the marinade ingredients together and pour the mixture over the chicken. Cover and stand for 1 hour. Then microwave on High for 16–18 minutes and stand for 3–4 minutes. Serve hot, or chill the drumsticks and serve cold.

VARIATION: To crisp the drumsticks, place them under a hot grill, or on the barbecue, for a few minutes — until they are brown and crisp. Baste them often with the marinade sauce.

Stuffed Roast Chicken (page 24) served with New Potatoes (page 40), Brussels Sprouts (page 36) and Vegetable Sauté (page 38).

CHEESY CRUMBED CHICKEN

This makes great picnic fare.

750 g/1½ lb chicken pieces
60 g/2 oz plain flour
1 egg, beaten
15 ml/1 tablespoon milk
salt and freshly ground black pepper to taste
60 g/2 oz dried breadcrumbs, seasoned
60 ml/4 tablespoons finely grated
   Parmesan or Cheddar cheese
20 ml/4 teaspoons oil

Dust the chicken with the flour. Mix the egg, milk and seasoning together. Mix the breadcrumbs and cheese together. Dip the chicken into the egg mixture, then coat with the breadcrumb and cheese mixture. Place the chicken on a plate and refrigerate for 30 minutes to firm the crust.

Preheat a browning dish on High for 8 minutes. Add the oil, then the chicken. Cover with a paper towel and microwave on High for 8 minutes, turning the chicken after 1 minute. Drain on a paper towel. Serve hot or cold.

CREAMY CHICKEN CURRY

Keep cooked chicken in the freezer so that a quick meal can be put together by defrosting the chicken and adding it to a sauce. Serve this curry on a bed of Savoury Rice (page 39).

30 g/1 oz butter
25 ml/5 teaspoons plain flour
5–10 ml/1–2 teaspoons curry powder
salt and freshly ground black pepper to taste
2.5 ml/½ teaspoon turmeric
200 ml/6½ fl oz hot chicken stock
155 ml/¼ pint single cream or plain yoghurt
1.5 kg/3 lb cooked chicken, chopped
grapes or sultanas and toasted almond
   flakes to garnish

Microwave the butter in a glass bowl on High for 1 minute. Stir in the flour, curry powder, seasoning and turmeric. Add the stock, stirring. Microwave on High for 4–5 minutes, stirring twice — until the sauce thickens. Add the cream or yoghurt and chicken, and heat through on Medium for 4–5 minutes. Serve immediately, garnished with grapes or sultanas and almonds.

Chicken Drumsticks with Barbecue Marinade Sauce (page 24) and Cheesy Crumbed Chicken (this page).

BAKED HONEY CHICKEN

This dish may be made in advance and then heated through just before serving.

    6–8 chicken pieces
    125 ml/4 fl oz dry sherry
    125 g/4 oz clear honey
    2 cloves garlic, crushed
    30 ml/2 tablespoons lemon juice
    25 ml/5 teaspoons soy sauce
    12.5/2½ teaspoons cornflour
    45 ml/3 tablespoons water
    salt and freshly ground black pepper to taste

Place the chicken in a casserole. Combine the sherry, honey, garlic, lemon juice and soy sauce, and pour over the chicken. Cover and microwave on Medium–High for 15 minutes — until the chicken is cooked. Remove the chicken, reserving the cooking juices, and cover to keep warm while making the sauce.

Combine the cornflour and water, and stir in some of the cooking juices. Stir this mixture into the rest of the cooking juices in the casserole. Season. Microwave on High for 2–3 minutes, stirring a few times — until the sauce thickens to the desired consistency. Pour the sauce over the chicken and serve.

VARIATION: In place of sherry, use a fruit juice, such as apricot, pineapple or orange.

APRICOT CHICKEN CASSEROLE

The easiest casserole you will ever make! Serve with rice.

    375 ml/12 fl oz apricot juice
    60 g/2 oz brown onion soup powder
    1 kg/2 lb chicken pieces

Mix the apricot juice and onion soup powder together in a jug. Put the chicken into a casserole and pour the liquid over. Cover and microwave on Medium–High for 20–25 minutes. Stir well, then serve.

HINT
Before barbecuing marinated poultry or meat, microwave, covered on High for 5 minutes. This helps the marinade to permeate the flesh and, as the poultry or meat is also slightly pre-cooked at the same time, it reduces barbecuing time. The result is crisp succulent chicken, or deliciously tender meat.

CHICKEN WITH MUSHROOMS

Succulent chicken cooked in a creamy mushroom sauce.

    4–8 chicken breasts
    60 g/2 oz brown onion soup powder
    200 ml/6½ fl oz water
    125 ml/4 fl oz soured cream or plain
      yoghurt
    75 ml/2½ fl oz medium dry sherry
    200 g/6½ oz button mushrooms, sliced
    chopped parsley to garnish

Weigh the chicken breasts and arrange them in a shallow dish. Mix the onion soup powder and water together in a jug and microwave on High for 2 minutes. Stir well, mix in the soured cream or yoghurt, sherry and mushrooms and pour the sauce over the chicken. Microwave, covered, on Medium–High for 15 minutes per 500 g/1 lb of chicken. Stand for a few minutes, then serve with rice, garnished with parsley.

SPICY CHICKEN LIVERS

Serve this healthy and tasty casserole on spaghetti.

    12.5/2½ teaspoons oil
    1 onion, chopped
    1 clove garlic, crushed
    250 g/8 oz chicken livers, cleaned (see
      Hint, page 6)
    12.5 ml/2½ teaspoons plain flour
    pinch of both turmeric and black pepper
    2.5 ml/½ teaspoon chilli powder
    5 ml/1 teaspoon salt
    20 ml/4 teaspoons soft brown sugar
    1 bayleaf
    5 ml/1 teaspoon vinegar
    12.5 ml/2½ teaspoons soy sauce
    25 ml/5 teaspoons tomato paste
    chopped parsley to garnish

Preheat a browning dish on High for 8 minutes. Add the oil, onion and garlic. Microwave on High for 2 minutes. Cut the chicken livers in half, dredge in flour, then add to the browning dish. Microwave on High for 2–3 minutes, stirring twice. Stir in the turmeric, pepper, chilli powder, salt, sugar, bayleaf, vinegar, soy sauce and tomato paste. Microwave on Medium–High for 6 minutes. Remove the bayleaf, then serve, garnished with parsley.

VARIATION: Add 200 g/6½ oz button mushrooms, sliced, with all the spices.

Stuffed Cabbage Rolls (page 30) and Meatballs in Tomato Sauce (page 30).

CHAPTER SEVEN

Meat

MEAT is an excellent source of protein, as well as a good source of minerals and trace elements. When cooked correctly in a microwave, meat is tender, tasty and succulent. This collection of dishes includes recipes for beef, lamb and pork.

NOTES

◆ Always use the best quality meat.
◆ Defrost meat completely before cooking.
◆ Tougher cuts of meat require long, slow cooking and brown beautifully. If cooking time is limited, a browning dish is essential to brown the meat. Never overload the browning dish as the meat will stew instead of browning.
◆ Never salt meat before cooking as it tends to draw out the juices, making the meat dry and tough.

MEAT LOAF

The secret is not to overmix the ingredients but to blend them lightly with a knife. Serve hot with mashed potato and vegetables, or cool and then freeze slices for lunch boxes (see Note).

MEAT LOAF
1 onion, chopped
25 ml/5 teaspoons water
500 g/1 lb lean minced beef
2 slices white or brown bread, crumbed
15 ml/1 tablespoon chopped parsley
5 ml/1 teaspoon dried thyme
2.5 ml/½ teaspoon freshly grated nutmeg
5 ml/1 teaspoon salt
2.5 ml/½ teaspoon freshly ground black pepper
10 ml/2 teaspoons vinegar
5 ml/1 teaspoon caster sugar
5 ml/1 teaspoon Worcestershire sauce
1 egg, beaten

GLAZE
45 ml/3 tablespoons fruit chutney
45 ml/3 tablespoons tomato ketchup
15 ml/1 tablespoon soft brown sugar
5 ml/1 teaspoon prepared mustard

In a small bowl, microwave the onion and water on High for 3 minutes. Drain. Mix the rest of the ingredients for the meat loaf together lightly with the onion, and spoon the mixture into a 1-kg/2–lb loaf pan. Press down. Mix the ingredients for the glaze together and brush the mixture over the meat loaf. Microwave on Medium-High for 10–12 minutes. Stand for 5 minutes, then turn out the meat loaf and slice to serve.

NOTE: To freeze, wrap individual slices in cling film. Defrost slices as needed.

CHILLI CON CARNE

Serve with wholemeal bread and a crisp green salad.

1 onion, chopped
2 rashers lean bacon, chopped
315 g/10 oz lean minced beef
15 ml/1 tablespoon semolina
100 g/3½ oz mushrooms, finely chopped
5 ml/1 teaspoon chilli powder
5 ml/1 teaspoon dried oregano
30 ml/2 tablespoons tomato paste
410 g/13 oz canned chopped tomatoes
freshly ground black pepper to taste
30 ml/2 tablespoons beef stock or water
2.5 ml/½ teaspoon caster sugar
5 ml/1 teaspoon malt vinegar
410 g/13 oz canned red kidney beans, drained

Preheat a browning dish on High for 8 minutes. Add the onion and bacon. Cover and microwave on High for 1 minute. Add the minced beef, stir, then microwave on High for 3 minutes. Add the remaining ingredients, except the beans. Stir well, cover and microwave on Medium for 12 minutes. Add the beans and microwave on High for 5 minutes. Stir and serve.

MEATBALLS IN TOMATO SAUCE

MEATBALLS
500 g/1 lb lean minced beef
1 medium onion, chopped
1 clove garlic, crushed
45 g/1½ oz fresh breadcrumbs
12.5 ml/2½ teaspoons chopped parsley
5 ml/1 teaspoon dried mixed herbs
1 egg, beaten
5 ml/1 teaspoon salt
good pinch of pepper

TOMATO SAUCE
410 g/15 oz canned condensed tomato
    soup
125 ml/¼ fl oz hot beef stock

chopped parsley to garnish

Mix all the ingredients for the meatballs together. Shape into medium-sized meatballs and arrange in a shallow casserole. Microwave the soup and stock for the sauce together in a jug on High for 3 minutes. Stir and pour over the meatballs. Microwave on High for about 15 minutes — or until cooked. Stand for about 5 minutes, then serve, garnished with parsley, with Buttered Noodles (below).

BUTTERED NOODLES

220 g/7 oz egg noodles
1 litre/1¾ pints boiling water
5 ml/1 teaspoon salt
5 ml/1 teaspoon oil
butter to taste

Place the noodles, water, salt and oil in a large bowl and microwave on High for about 8 minutes — until the noodles are al dente. Stand for 5 minutes, drain, then dot with butter and serve.

STUFFED CABBAGE ROLLS

8 medium cabbage leaves, washed
30 g/1 oz butter
1 small onion, chopped
450 g/14 oz lean minced beef
100 g/3½ oz button mushrooms, chopped
5 ml/1 teaspoon Worcestershire sauce
salt and freshly ground black pepper to taste
410 g/13 oz canned cream of tomato soup

Place the still wet cabbage leaves on the turntable and microwave on High for about 2 minutes — until they soften. Microwave the butter and onion in a bowl on High for 3 minutes. Add the mince and microwave on High for 3 minutes, stirring to break it up. Add the mushrooms, Worcestershire sauce and seasoning, and microwave on High for 2 minutes. Place a portion of the filling in the centre of each cabbage leaf. Fold the sides over and roll the leaves up so that the filling is completely enclosed. Place the rolls, seam-side down, in a shallow casserole. Pour the soup over the rolls. Cover and microwave on High for 10–12 minutes. Stand for 3–4 minutes, then serve.

CHEESE AND HAM MEAT ROLL

500 g/1 lb minced beef
salt and freshly ground black pepper to taste
2.5 ml/½ teaspoon ground coriander
pinch of ground cloves
25 ml/5 teaspoons tomato paste
2 eggs
30 g/1 oz fresh breadcrumbs
12.5 ml/2½ teaspoons soy sauce
200 g/6½ oz cooked ham slices
100 g/3½ oz Cheddar cheese, grated
25 ml/5 teaspoons chutney
12.5 ml/2½ teaspoons chopped parsley

Mix the mince, seasoning and spices, tomato paste, eggs, breadcrumbs and soy sauce together lightly. Cover a Swiss roll tin with cling film so that the cling film overlaps the edges. Fill the tin with the mince mixture and press down well. Arrange the ham slices on top and sprinkle with cheese. Roll up like a Swiss roll with the aid of the cling film. Smear the top of the roll with chutney and sprinkle with parsley. Place the roll in a glass dish, seam-side down. Microwave on Medium–High for 15 minutes. Serve hot or cold.

VARIATIONS: Replace the ham with a tomato and onion mixture or chopped, sautéed onions and mushrooms.

COOKING STEAK
Use this chart as a guide to cooking time on High for steak per side in a preheated browning dish:

	1 STEAK	2 STEAKS	3 STEAKS	4 STEAKS
RARE	1 min.	1½ min.	2 min.	2½ min.
MEDIUM	1½ min.	1¾ min.	2¼ min.	3½ min.
WELL-DONE	2 min.	2½ min.	3 min.	3½ min.

Apricot Sausage Kebabs (page 33) with Savoury Rice (page 39)

STEAKS WITH MUSHROOM SAUCE

4 beef steaks
5 ml/1 teaspoon garlic salt
12.5 ml/2½ teaspoons each oil and butter

MUSHROOM SAUCE
1 onion, chopped
200 g/6½ oz mushrooms, sliced
1 clove garlic, crushed
30 ml/2 tablespoons sherry
100 ml/3½ fl oz hot beef stock
7.5 ml/1½ teaspoons tomato paste
25 ml/5 teaspoons cornflour
45 ml/3 tablespoons single cream

Preheat a browning dish on High for 8 minutes. Pat the meat dry and press in the seasoning. Add the oil and butter to the browning dish, then add the steaks. Microwave on High for 2½–3 minutes (see chart on page 30). Remove the steaks, reserving the cooking juices, and cover to keep warm while making the sauce.

To make the sauce, add the onion, mushrooms and garlic to the cooking juices. Microwave on High for 4–5 minutes — until soft. Add the sherry, stock and tomato paste. Mix the cornflour with a little water and stir in. Microwave on High for 2–3 minutes. Stir in the cream before serving.

DEVILLED SWISS STEAK

60 g/2 oz plain flour
12.5 ml/2½ teaspoons mustard powder
2.5 ml/½ teaspoon pepper
500 g/1 lb stewing steak, cubed
15 ml/1 tablespoon oil
2 onions, sliced
410 g/13 oz canned chopped tomatoes
45 ml/3 tablespoons Worcestershire sauce
15 ml/1 tablespoon soft brown sugar
5 ml/1 teaspoon chilli sauce

Mix the flour, mustard and pepper together. Roll the steak pieces in flour. Preheat a browning dish on High for 8 minutes. Add the oil and steak and microwave on High for 4 minutes, stirring after 2 minutes. Remove the steak, add the onions to the dish and microwave on High for 4 minutes. Add the tomatoes and liquid, Worcestershire sauce, brown sugar and chilli sauce, then mix in the meat. Cover and microwave on Medium-Low for 35–40 minutes — until tender. Stand for about 10 minutes, then serve with rice.

COMBINATION OVEN: Cook at 160 °C temperature and low microwave power level for 40 minutes (or for 60 minutes if your oven alternates between both convection and microwave energy).

SIMPLE LAMB CHOPS

Serve with new potatoes tossed in butter and a green salad.

12.5/2½ teaspoons oil
5 ml/1 teaspoon lemon juice
2.5 ml/½ teaspoon chopped fresh rosemary
pinch of caster sugar
4 lamb chops

Combine the oil, lemon juice, rosemary and sugar, and marinate the chops in the mixture for 30 minutes or longer. Preheat a browning dish on High for 8 minutes. Remove the chops from the marinade and place in the browning dish. Microwave on High for 2¾ minutes per side (see chart on page 33). Serve.

VARIATION: For Crumbed Lamb Chops, dip the chops in seasoned flour (see Hint, right), then beaten egg, and then breadcrumbs. Refrigerate for at least 30 minutes. Heat 20 ml/4 teaspoons oil in a pre-heated browning dish on High for 1 minute, then microwave chops according to chart (see page 33).

DEVILLED LAMB CHOPS

4 lamb chump chops
25 ml/5 teaspoons chutney
5 ml/1 teaspoon curry powder
10 ml/2 teaspoons soft brown sugar
7.5 ml/1½ teaspoons soy sauce
5 ml/1 teaspoon red wine vinegar

Use a sharp knife to make deep cuts in the fat, then pat the chops dry with a paper towel. Preheat a browning dish on High for 8 minutes. Add the chops and microwave on High for 2¾ minutes on each side. Remove the chops and add the remaining ingredients to the dish. Stir well to mix. Microwave on High for 1½ minutes. Pour the sauce over the chops and serve.

HINT

To make seasoned flour, add a pinch of dried mixed herbs and freshly ground black pepper to 25 ml/5 teaspoons plain flour.

Simple Lamb Chops (this page), and Veal Schnitzels with Creamy Mustard Sauce (page 33) served with Tomatoes, Onions and Mushrooms with Sherry (page 38).

VEAL SCHNITZELS WITH CREAMY MUSTARD SAUCE

4 large veal schnitzels
30 ml/2 tablespoons plain flour
30 ml/2 tablespoons grated Parmesan cheese
2.5 ml/½ teaspoon salt
2.5 ml/½ teaspoon freshly ground black
   pepper
1 egg, beaten
30 g/1 oz dried breadcrumbs, seasoned

CREAMY MUSTARD SAUCE
30 g/1 oz butter
30 ml/2 tablespoons plain flour
200 ml/6½ fl oz single cream
100 ml/3½ fl oz hot beef stock
10 ml/2 teaspoons lemon juice
2.5 ml/½ teaspoon salt
good pinch of black pepper
7.5 ml/1½ teaspoons Dijon mustard

12.5 ml/2½ teaspoons oil
12.5 ml/2½ teaspoons butter

Place the schnitzels between two layers of cling film and flatten slightly with a mallet. Combine the flour, cheese, salt and pepper and coat the schnitzels with the mixture. Dip the schnitzels in the egg and then coat with the breadcrumbs. Refrigerate for 30 minutes.

To make the sauce, microwave the butter in a jug or bowl on High for 30 seconds. Stir in the flour and blend well. Gradually stir in the cream, stock and lemon juice. Microwave on High for 3 minutes, stirring a few times. Add the salt, pepper and mustard. Keep the sauce warm.

Preheat a browning dish on High for 8 minutes. Add the oil and butter, then the schnitzels. Microwave on High for 4 minutes, turning after 1 minute. Pour the sauce over the schnitzels to serve.

VARIATION: To make Paprika Sauce, add 1 onion, chopped, to the butter and microwave on High for 3 minutes. Stir in 10 ml/2 teaspoons paprika with the flour, and omit the lemon juice and mustard.

COOKING LAMB CHOPS

Use this chart as a guide to cooking time for chops per side on High in a browning dish:

1 CHOP	2 CHOPS	3 CHOPS	4 CHOPS
1½ min.	1¾ min.	2¼ min.	2¾ min.

LIVER AND ONIONS

Serve with mashed potato or Buttered Noodles (page 30) and vegetables of your choice.

500 g/1 lb lamb's liver, cleaned and
   skinned (see Note)
45 ml/3 tablespoons seasoned flour (see
   Hint, page 32)
25 ml/5 teaspoons oil
30 g/1 oz butter
1 large onion, thinly sliced
2.5 ml/½ teaspoon dried mixed herbs
250 ml/8 fl oz hot beef stock
15 ml/1 tablespoon gravy powder

Cut the liver into thin slices, pat dry and dust with seasoned flour. Preheat a browning dish on High for 8 minutes. Add the oil and butter, then the onion and liver. Microwave on High for 3–4 minutes. Stir, then microwave on High for another 2 minutes — until the liver is cooked. Remove the liver and onions from the dish, and add the herbs and stock. Microwave on High for 2 minutes. Blend the gravy powder with a little water and add to the stock. Stir well and then microwave on High for 2–3 minutes, stirring twice — until thickened. Add the liver and onions to the gravy and microwave on High for 2–3 minutes to heat through. Serve as suggested.

NOTE: To prepare lamb's liver for cooking, wipe the liver with a cloth, then remove the membrane and veining with a sharp knife.

APRICOT SAUSAGE KEBABS

These kebabs are so easy to make! Serve them on a bed of Savoury Rice (page 39) for a simple but tasty meal.

500 g/1 lb rindless streaky bacon
100 g/3½ oz dried apricots
6 pork sausages, each cut into 3 pieces
8 wooden kebab sticks

Cut each bacon rasher into three pieces. Wrap the apricots and sausage pieces in bacon, then thread alternately on to kebab sticks. Place the kebabs on a bacon rack, and microwave on High for 6 minutes (or for 4 minutes if you are cooking 4 kebabs at a time). Leave to stand for 2 minutes, then serve.

VARIATIONS: Use large Frankfurters or a chunky smoked variety. To make mini-kebabs, thread small pieces of sausage and halved dried apricots on to cocktail sticks.

PORK FILLET IN BROWN ONION AND APPLE SAUCE

The easiest of dishes to make.

> 60 g/2 oz brown onion soup powder
> 200 ml/6½ fl oz apple juice
> 100 ml/3½ fl oz water
> 750 g/1½ lb pork fillet, sliced in large pieces

Mix the onion soup powder, apple juice and water in a jug. Place the pork fillet pieces in a cooking bag (or in a covered casserole). Pour the liquid into the bag, tie a loose knot and place in a dish (to collect the juices if they spill out). Microwave on High for 5 minutes, then on Medium-High for 8–10 minutes. Stand for 2–3 minutes before serving.

COMBINATION OVEN: Cook at 200 °C temperature and medium-low microwave power level for 12 minutes (18–20 minutes if your oven alternates convection and microwave energy).

PORK FILLETS IN MUSHROOMS SAUCE

> 4 pork fillets (about 625 g/1¼ lb)
> 25 ml/5 teaspoons oil
>
> MUSHROOM SAUCE
> 1 onion, chopped
> 200 g/6½ oz button mushrooms, quartered
> 12.5 ml/2½ teaspoons chopped parsley
> 5 ml/1 teaspoon dried mixed herbs
> 30 g/1 oz butter
> 30 ml/2 tablespoons plain flour
> 25 ml/5 teaspoons tomato paste
> 170 ml/5½ fl oz hot chicken stock
> 125 ml/4 fl oz rosé wine
> salt and freshly ground black pepper to taste

Pat the pork fillets dry with a paper towel. Preheat a browning dish on High for 8 minutes. Add the oil, then the pork fillets. Microwave on High for 2 minutes, then turn over and microwave on High for 4–6 minutes. Set aside and keep warm.

To make the sauce, add the onions, mushrooms, parsley and mixed herbs to the dish. Cover and microwave on High for 5 minutes. Stir in the butter, then the flour. Add the tomato paste, chicken stock and wine. Microwave on High for 3 minutes, stirring twice. Season, then add the pork fillets to the sauce, coating them in the sauce. Cover and microwave on High for 3–4 minutes to heat through.

SWEET AND SOUR PORK

> 15 ml/1 tablespoon oil
> 750 g/1½ lb loin or shoulder of pork, cubed
> 250 ml/8 fl oz pineapple juice
> 125 ml/4 fl oz hot water or chicken stock
> 75 ml/2½ fl oz red wine vinegar
> 60 ml/4 tablespoons dark brown sugar
> 25 ml/5 teaspoons cornflour
> 25 ml/5 teaspoons soy sauce
> 5 ml/1 teaspoon Worcestershire sauce
> 185 g/6 oz pineapple chunks
> ½ green pepper, seeded and diced
> ½ onion, chopped

Preheat a browning dish on High for 8 minutes. Add the oil, then the pork and microwave on High for 2 minutes. Turn and microwave on High for another 3 minutes. Remove the pork and drain.

Mix the pineapple juice, water or stock, vinegar, sugar, cornflour, soy and Worcestershire sauces together in a jug. Stir to dissolve the cornflour, then microwave on High for 2–3 minutes — until thickened.

Wipe the browning dish, add the pork and sauce, cover and microwave on Medium-Low for 25 minutes. Add the pineapple, green pepper and onion. Microwave, uncovered, on High for 5 minutes. Serve.

PORK CHOPS NORMANDY

> APPLE SAUCE
> 1 onion, chopped
> 22 g/¾ oz butter
> 1 Granny Smith apple, peeled, cored and diced
> 25 ml/5 teaspoons plain flour
> 10 ml/2 teaspoons lemon juice
> 2.5 ml/½ teaspoon salt
> freshly ground black pepper to taste
> 100 ml/3½ fl oz apple juice
> 60 ml/4 tablespoons dry white wine
> 45 ml/3 tablespoons hot chicken stock
>
> 4 rib or loin pork chops (about 500 g/1 lb)

To make the sauce, microwave the onion and butter in a bowl on High for 3 minutes. Add the apple and microwave on High for 1 minute. Stir in the flour, then the remaining ingredients for the sauce. Microwave on High for 3–4 minutes, stirring twice — until the sauce thickens. Keep warm.

Preheat a browning dish on High for 8 minutes. Pat the chops dry and make deep cuts in the fat with a sharp knife. Microwave in the browning dish on High for 2½ minutes per side. Serve with apple sauce.

Sweet and Sour Pork (page 34) with Vegetable Stir-Fry (page 38).

CHAPTER EIGHT

Vegetables & rice

VEGETABLES are superb cooked in a microwave. They require very little water and no salt (a health advantage) so the nutritional content is preserved and the cooked vegetables have wonderful colour, texture and taste. Rice also cooks well in the microwave.

NOTES
◆ Seal containers with pierced cling film or a tight-fitting lid to keep the steam in when cooking vegetables.
◆ Chop vegetables into uniform-sized pieces to ensure even cooking.

BROCCOLI SURPRISE

A delicious way to prepare this nutritious vegetable.

> 375 g/12 oz broccoli florets, trimmed
> 30 ml/2 tablespoons water
> 12.5 ml/2½ teaspoons butter
> 1 clove garlic, crushed
> pinch of dried tarragon
> 2.5 ml/½ teaspoon prepared mustard
> 5 ml/1 teaspoon lemon juice
> 2.5 ml/½ teaspoon grated lemon zest
> freshly ground black pepper to taste

Soak the broccoli in water to cover for 30 minutes. Drain, then microwave with the 30 ml/2 tablespoons water in a glass bowl, covered, on High for 5–6 minutes — until just cooked (the colour will be a beautiful green). Drain. Place the remaining ingredients in a ramekin or cup and microwave on High for 30–40 seconds. Pour the mixture over the broccoli and serve.

BRUSSELS SPROUTS

> 375 g/12 oz Brussels sprouts
> 30 ml/2 tablespoons water
> 10 ml/2 teaspoons butter
> pinch of freshly grated nutmeg
> 10 ml/2 teaspoons lemon juice

Cut off the stems and outer leaves of the sprouts. Soak in water for 15 minutes. Drain and cut a cross in the stem end of each sprout. Place the sprouts in a bowl with the water, cover tightly and microwave on High for 6–7 minutes. Drain, toss in the butter, and add the nutmeg and lemon juice. Serve.

CREAMED SPINACH

> 1 small onion, finely chopped
> 1 clove garlic, crushed
> 30 g/1 oz butter
> 250 g/8 oz frozen spinach, thawed and drained
> 100 ml/3½ fl oz soured cream
> freshly ground black pepper to taste

Place the onion, garlic and butter in a bowl and microwave on High for 3 minutes. Add the spinach, soured cream and pepper. Microwave on Medium for 4–5 minutes — until hot. Serve.

BAKED BUTTERNUT SQUASH

> 500 g/1 lb butternut squash, peeled and sliced into rounds
> 5 ml/1 teaspoon ground cinnamon
> 25 ml/5 teaspoons soft brown sugar
> 22 g/¾ oz butter

Layer the butternut squash rounds, overlapping, in a shallow casserole. Sprinkle with cinnamon and sugar. Melt the butter on High for 20 seconds and pour over the butternut squash. Microwave, covered, on High for 10 minutes. Stand for 2–3 minutes, then serve.

VARIATION: Use pumpkin instead of squash.

Broccoli Surprise (page 36), Carrots with Soured Cream (this page) and Cauliflower Bake (this page).

CAULIFLOWER BAKE

375 g/12 oz cauliflower florets, trimmed
30 ml/2 tablespoons water
410 g/13 oz canned cream of mushroom soup
60 g/2 oz Cheddar cheese, grated
45 ml/3 tablespoons mayonnaise
45 ml/3 tablespoons milk
1 egg, beaten
30 g/1 oz fresh wholemeal breadcrumbs
20 ml/4 teaspoons butter, melted
paprika to taste

Soak the cauliflower in water to cover for 30 minutes. Drain, then microwave with the 30 ml/2 tablespoons water in a bowl, covered, on High for 5–6 minutes — until just cooked. Drain. Mix together the soup, cheese, mayonnaise, milk and egg. Pour the mixture over the cauliflower. Mix the breadcrumbs and butter together and sprinkle on top. Dust with paprika, then microwave on Medium-High for 8–10 minutes. Serve piping hot.

VARIATIONS
◆ Use broccoli instead of cauliflower.
◆ Spoon a layer of a whole cooked and chopped chicken into a pie dish. Top with Cauliflower Bake. Microwave on High for 2–3 minutes to heat through, then serve.

CARROTS WITH SOURED CREAM

250 g/8 oz carrots, peeled and sliced
12.5 ml/2½ teaspoons dry white wine or water
freshly ground black pepper to taste
75 ml/2½ fl oz soured cream
5 ml/1 teaspoon chopped fresh dill or parsley

Microwave the carrots and wine or water in a bowl, covered, on High for 5–6 minutes – until the carrots are tender. Stir in the pepper, soured cream and dill or parsley. Serve hot or cold.

COURGETTE SAUTE

8 courgettes, sliced
45 g/1½ oz butter
75 ml/2½ fl oz dry white wine
5 ml/1 teaspoon chopped fresh thyme
2.5 ml/½ teaspoon salt (optional)

Microwave the courgettes and butter in a glass bowl on High for 2 minutes. Stir, then add the wine and thyme. Microwave, covered, on High for 4–5 minutes, stirring twice. Add the salt, if using, and serve.

VEGETABLE SAUTE

All vegetables are medium-sized.

> 2 carrots, peeled and cut in julienne strips
> 1 potato, peeled and cut in julienne strips
> 1 leek, cut in julienne strips
> 1 turnip, peeled and cut in julienne strips
> 2 sticks celery, cut in julienne strips
> 30 g/1 oz butter
> freshly ground black pepper to taste
> 45 ml/3 tablespoons bean sprouts
> chopped parsley to garnish

Place the vegetables, butter and pepper in a dish. Cover and microwave on High for 5–7 minutes. Stir in the bean sprouts, garnish with parsley and serve.

VARIATIONS: Use any vegetables of your choice. A selection of fresh and tender baby vegetables is good.

VEGETABLE STIR-FRY

Don't cover the vegetables or add water as they cook in their own juices.

> 45 ml/3 tablespoons oil
> 2 cloves garlic, crushed
> 1 large onion, sliced
> 10 ml/2 teaspoons grated fresh ginger
> 3 carrots, peeled and cut in julienne strips
> 3 sticks celery, cut in julienne strips
> 1 red pepper, seeded and cut in julienne
>   strips
> 200 g/6½ oz cabbage, finely shredded
> 30 ml/2 tablespoons sherry
> 30 ml/2 tablespoons soy sauce
> 45 ml/3 tablespoons bean sprouts

Preheat a browning dish on High for 8 minutes. Add the oil, garlic, onion and ginger. Stir and microwave on High for 3 minutes. Add the carrot, celery, red pepper and cabbage. Stir well and microwave on High for 4 minutes, stirring twice. Add the sherry, soy sauce and bean sprouts. Stir well and microwave on High for 1–2 minutes. Serve immediately.

HINT
To dégorge aubergine, place cubed aubergine in a colander. Sprinkle generously with salt and leave to stand for 30 minutes to draw out the bitter juices. Wash well under cold running water, pat dry thoroughly and use.

TOMATOES, ONIONS AND MUSHROOMS WITH SHERRY

Serve with Meat Loaf (page 29) or steak (see page 31).

> 345 g/11 oz pickling onions, peeled
> 30 g/1 oz butter
> 100 ml/3½ fl oz sherry
> 200 g/6½ oz small button mushrooms
> 15 ml/1 tablespoon tomato paste
> 155 g/5 oz cherry tomatoes, peeled (see
>   Hint, page 17)
> freshly ground black pepper to taste
> pinch of caster sugar

Preheat a browning dish on High for 8 minutes. Add the onions and butter. Microwave on High for 3 minutes, stirring once. Pour in the sherry. Cover and microwave on High for 3 minutes. Mix in the remaining ingredients. Microwave on High for 2–3 minutes — until cooked. Serve as suggested.

HINT
To peel onions easily, pour boiling water over to cover, leave for 5 minutes, then drain, rinse and peel.

RATATOUILLE

> 1 small aubergine, diced and dégorged
>   (see Hint, left)
> 15 g/½ oz butter
> 1 small onion, chopped
> 1 clove garlic, crushed
> ½ green pepper, seeded and diced
> 1 large tomato, peeled and chopped (see
>   Hint, page 17)
> 90 g/3 oz courgettes, sliced
> 15 ml/1 tablespoon tomato paste
> pinch of dried oregano
> freshly ground black pepper to taste
> 15 ml/1 tablespoon chopped parsley
> few black olives, pitted (optional)
> dash of soured cream (optional)

Mix the aubergine with the butter, onion, garlic and green pepper in a bowl. Microwave on High for 3–4 minutes. Stir in the tomato, courgette, tomato paste and herbs. Season and microwave on High for 5–6 minutes, stirring twice — until vegetables are soft. Sprinkle with parsley, add a few olives, if using, and drizzle soured cream over, if using, just before serving.

Braised Red Cabbage (page 41), Fan Potatoes (page 40) and Honey-Baked Sweet Potatoes (page 41).

SAVOURY RICE

    30 g/1 oz butter
    1 onion, chopped
    1 green pepper, seeded and chopped
    2.5 ml/½ teaspoon each dried sage,
       dried basil and dried oregano
    5 ml/1 teaspoon each salt and pepper
    200 g/6½ oz white rice, cooked (see below)

In a small glass bowl, microwave the butter, onion, and green pepper on High for 2 minutes. Add the herbs and seasoning. Mix into the rice. Microwave on High for 2 minutes, then serve.

COOKING RICE
◆ To cook 200 g/6½ oz WHITE RICE, add 500–750 ml/ 16–24 fl oz boiling water and 5 ml/1 teaspoon salt. Microwave, covered, on High for 10–15 minutes, then stand for 15 minutes.
◆ To cook 200 g/6½ oz BROWN RICE, add 500–625 ml/ 16–20 fl oz boiling water and 5 ml/1 teaspoon salt. Microwave, covered, on High for 25–30 minutes, then stand for 15 minutes.
◆ Reheat rice, covered, on High for 5–6 minutes.

APPLE AND COURGETTE SALAD

    500 g/1 lb courgettes, sliced
    45 ml/3 tablespoons water
    75 ml/2½ fl oz oil
    15 ml/1 tablespoon fresh lemon juice
    25 ml/5 teaspoons wine vinegar
    5 ml/1 teaspoon caster sugar
    5 ml/1 teaspoon dried basil
    2.5 ml/½ teaspoon salt
    25 ml/5 teaspoons chopped parsley
    freshly ground black pepper to taste
    3 apples, cored and diced
    1 onion, thinly sliced
    1 green pepper, seeded and cut in
       julienne strips

Microwave the courgettes and water in a bowl, covered, on High for 3 minutes. Stand, then drain. Blend the oil, lemon juice, vinegar, sugar, basil, salt, parsley and pepper in a food processor for a few seconds (or shake in a screw-topped jar). Pour into a large serving bowl. Add the apple and mix well. Mix in the onion, green pepper and courgettes. Cover and chill before serving.

VARIATION: Instead of courgettes, use a mixture of sliced carrots, blanched broccoli florets and cubes of peeled or unpeeled cucumber.

Creamed Spinach (page 36), Ratatouille (page 38) and Cheesy Baked Potatoes (page 41).

NEW POTATOES

> 500 g/1 lb new potatoes, scrubbed
> 45 ml/3 tablespoons water
> 30 g/1 oz butter
> 15 ml/1 tablespoon chopped parsley

Microwave the potatoes and water in a small bowl, covered, on High for 8–10 minutes — until tender. Stand for 5 minutes, then drain. Microwave the butter on High for 20 seconds. Sprinkle the potatoes with the parsley, pour the butter over and serve.

BAKED POTATOES

MEDIUM POTATOES	COOKING TIME ON HIGH
1	3 min.
2	4–5 min.
3	6–7 min.
4	7–8 min.
5	10–12 min.

FAN POTATOES

> 4 medium potatoes, scrubbed (do not peel)
> 100 ml/3½ fl oz water
> 125 ml/4 fl oz milk
> 100 g/3½ oz butter
> 30 g/1 oz packet brown onion soup powder

Cut small slits in the potatoes, about 2 mm/⅛ inch apart, almost through to the base. Arrange the potatoes in a dish and pour the water over. Microwave, covered, on High for 5 minutes. Drain. Microwave the milk and butter in a jug on High for 1½ minutes — until the butter has melted. Add the soup powder and mix well. Pour the mixture over the potatoes slowly, coating each potato thoroughly. Microwave on High for about 8 minutes, basting often with the soup mixture. Stand for 2–3 minutes, then serve.

COMBINATION OVEN: Cook at 230 °C temperature and medium microwave power level for about 20 minutes (30 minutes if your oven alternates convection and microwave energy).

CHEESY BAKED POTATOES

Baked potatoes are a wonderful addition to any meal.
Follow a few rules for perfect results.

    4 medium potatoes, scrubbed (do not peel)
    60 g/2 oz Cheddar cheese, grated
    chopped parsley to garnish

Prick the potatoes with a sharp knife. Place on a paper towel on the turntable, spacing evenly. Microwave on High for 7–8 minutes, turning after 3–4 minutes. They should yield slightly to finger pressure when ready (as they continue cooking during standing time). Stand for at least 5 minutes, during which time they will soften. (Wrap in foil, shiny-side inside, to keep warm for up to 30 minutes before eating.) To serve, cut a cross in each potato and squeeze open gently. Top with the grated cheese and garnish with parsley.

VARIATIONS
Add any of these toppings to each potato:
◆ savoury butter, like garlic or herb, of your choice;
◆ soured cream, double cream or cottage cheese (plain or a savoury variety);
◆ crumbled blue cheese mixed with a little soured cream.

Garnish with any of the following:
◆ snipped fresh chives or chopped spring onion;
◆ seasoned salt or paprika.

CHEESY ONION AND POTATO BAKE

This is so quick to put together and tastes delicious!

    500 g/1 lb potatoes, peeled and sliced
    100 ml/3½ fl oz water
    60 g/2 oz thick white onion soup powder
    410 ml/13 fl oz boiling water
    100 ml/3½ fl oz single cream or plain
        yoghurt
    60 g/2 oz Cheddar cheese, grated
    pinch of paprika
    chopped parsley to garnish

Microwave the potatoes and the 100 ml/3½ fl oz water in a bowl, covered, on High for 5 minutes. Stand, then drain. Mix the soup powder and the 410 ml/13 fl oz boiling water together in a jug. Stand for a few minutes. Stir in the cream or yoghurt. Layer the potatoes and soup mixture in a pie dish. Sprinkle with cheese and paprika. Microwave on Medium-High for 15 minutes. Stand for 5 minutes, garnish with parsley and serve.

HONEY-BAKED SWEET POTATOES

    750 g/1½ lb sweet potatoes, scrubbed
    500 ml/16 fl oz water
    60 g/2 oz butter
    30 ml/2 tablespoons clear honey
    pinch of salt
    2.5 ml/½ teaspoon ground cinnamon

Pierce the skins of the sweet potatoes and place them in a glass dish with the water. Cover and microwave on High for 10 minutes. Stand for 5 minutes, then drain and peel. In a jug, microwave the butter, honey, salt and cinnamon on High for 1 minute. Slice the sweet potatoes and place in a pie dish. Pour the sauce over, then microwave on High for 8 minutes. Stand for 2–3 minutes, then serve.

BAKED SWEETCORN

    4 corn-on-the-cob
    15 g/½ oz butter
    pinch of salt or seasoning of your choice

Remove the husks and silk from the corn and wrap each cob in waxed paper. Place, evenly spaced, on the turntable and microwave on High for about 8 minutes. Stand for about 3 minutes, remove the waxed paper, spread the corn with butter and sprinkle with seasoning. Serve hot.

BRAISED RED CABBAGE

    1 small red cabbage, shredded
    100 ml/3½ fl oz water
    15 g/½ of butter
    12.5 ml/2½ teaspoons caster sugar
    1 onion, chopped
    2 Granny Smith apples, peeled, cored
        and sliced
    30 ml/2 tablespoons apple cider vinegar
    freshly ground black pepper to taste

Microwave the cabbage and half the water in a bowl, covered, on High for 3–4 minutes. Set aside. Microwave the butter in a glass bowl on High for 30 seconds. Add the sugar and stir. Microwave on High for 1½–2 minutes — until golden brown. Add the onion and apples. Cover and microwave on High for 3 minutes. Add the cabbage, vinegar and remaining water. Mix well. Cover and microwave on Medium-High for 7–10 minutes — until the vegetables are tender. Season to taste and serve.

CHAPTER NINE

DESSERTS can be made easily and quickly in a microwave. A steamed pudding, which takes so long on the hob and requires constant attention, takes no more than 10 minutes in the microwave, with superb results. Light, fruity desserts are perfect in summer.

> **NOTE**
> Most desserts cook better on a low rack, which ensures that the centre sets, cooking is even and there is no build-up of steam at the base, which causes a sticky texture.

APRICOT CRISP

410 g/13 oz canned apricots, drained
   and syrup reserved
25 ml/5 teaspoons custard powder
12.5 ml/2½ teaspoons sherry

CRUMBLE TOPPING
125 g/4 oz plain flour
pinch of salt
90 g/3 oz butter
60 g/2 oz soft brown sugar
60 g/2 oz pecan nuts, coarsely chopped
45 g/1½ oz oats
5 ml/1 teaspoon ground cinnamon

Mix a little of the apricot syrup with the custard powder. Add the remaining syrup. Microwave on High for 2 minutes — until thick. Stir, then add the sherry. Layer the apricots in a pie dish and cover with the hot custard and sherry sauce.

To make the topping, sift the flour and salt together and rub in the butter (or blend in food processor). Mix in the sugar, nuts and oats. Sprinkle the crumble mixture over the apricots and dust the top with cinnamon. Microwave the pie on Medium-High for 10–12 minutes. Stand for a few minutes, then serve.

COMBINATION OVEN: Cook at 200 °C temperature and medium-low microwave power level for 12–14 minutes (20–25 minutes if your oven alternates convection and microwave energy).

TWO GOOSEBERRIES PUDDING

This is a 'Please may I have some more?' kind of dessert that is so easy to make.

625 g/1¼ lb canned gooseberries,
   drained and syrup reserved
45 ml/3 tablespoons custard powder
25 ml/5 teaspoons granulated sugar
45 g/1½ oz butter
170 ml/5½ fl oz condensed milk
250 ml/8 fl oz single cream
25 ml/5 teaspoons caster sugar

Cape gooseberries (physalis) for
   decoration (optional)

Add water to the reserved gooseberry syrup to make it up to 500 ml/16 fl oz. Mix a little syrup with the custard powder and sugar, then mix into the rest of the syrup. Microwave on High for 5–6 minutes — until the mixture thickens. Stir in the butter and set aside to cool.

When the mixture has cooled, mix in the condensed milk and gooseberries, and spoon the pudding into a greased pie dish. Cool in the refrigerator.

Whip the cream and caster sugar together until stiff, then pipe on top of the cooled pie. Decorate with Cape gooseberries, if using.

VARIATIONS
◆ Use any fruit, such as apricots, strawberries or peaches, instead of gooseberries.
◆ To make a pie instead of a pudding, make a pie crust by mixing together 45 ml/3 tablespoons melted butter, 90 g/3 oz crushed digestive biscuits and 45 ml/3 tablespoons condensed milk and pressing the mixture into the base and sides of a 23-cm/9-inch greased pie dish. Microwave the pie crust on High for 1–2 minutes. Make the pudding mixture as described above and pour it into the pie crust. Decorate the pie in the same way as the pudding.

Two Gooseberries Pudding (page 42).

RHUBARB AND APPLE CRUMBLE

500 g/1 lb rhubarb
2 Granny Smith apples
10 ml/2 teaspoons lemon juice
45 g/1½ oz caster sugar
30 ml/2 tablespoons water or orange juice

CRUMBLE TOPPING
125 g/4 oz plain flour
5 ml/1 teaspoon baking powder
60 g/2 oz granulated sugar
pinch of salt
75 g/2½ oz butter

Wash and trim the rhubarb, and cut into 2.5-cm/1-inch pieces. Peel, core and slice the apples, then coat in lemon juice. Place the rhubarb, apples, sugar and water or orange juice in a bowl and microwave on High for about 6 minutes, stirring once. Taste to see if the fruit is sweet enough. If not, add a little more sugar and microwave on High for 1 minute. Spoon the mixture into a 23-cm/9-inch pie dish.

To make the topping, sift the dry ingredients into a bowl. Rub in the butter (or blend in a food processor), and crumble the mixture over the filling. Microwave the pie on High for 8–10 minutes. Serve warm.

COMBINATION OVEN: Cook on 200 °C temperature and medium-low microwave power level for 12–14 minutes (20–25 minutes if your oven alternates convection and microwave energy).

VARIATIONS
◆ Sprinkle 60 g/2 oz chopped hazelnuts over the topping before cooking.
◆ If using orange juice instead of water, add 5 ml/1 teaspoon grated orange zest to the topping mixture.

CUSTARD

25 ml/5 teaspoons custard powder
410 ml/13 fl oz milk
25 ml/5 teaspoons caster sugar

Mix the custard powder and a little milk into a paste. Pour the remaining milk into a large jug and microwave on High for 2 minutes. Stir in the sugar, then add to the custard paste. Stir well; microwave on High for about 4 minutes, stirring after 2 minutes — until it thickens. Serve hot, or cover the surface of the custard with greaseproof paper to prevent a skin from forming and allow to cool.
MAKES 410 ML/13 FL OZ.

BAKED CHOCOLATE PUDDING

The family will love this dessert! It is delicious with Custard (page 43), whipped cream or ice cream.

CHOCOLATE PUDDING
45 g/1½ oz butter
155 g/5 oz granulated sugar
1 egg
2.5 ml/½ teaspoon vanilla extract
125 g/4 oz plain flour
5 ml/1 teaspoon baking powder
20 ml/4 teaspoons cocoa powder
good pinch of salt
170 ml/5½ fl oz milk

CHOCOLATE SAUCE
315 ml/½ pint water
25 ml/5 teaspoons cocoa powder
200 g/6½ oz soft brown sugar

Cream the butter and sugar together. Beat the egg and vanilla extract into the creamed mixture. Sift the dry ingredients and add, alternately with the milk, to the creamed mixture. Mix well. Spoon the pudding batter into a greased 20-cm/8-inch soufflé dish.

Place the ingredients for the sauce in a glass bowl or jug and microwave on High for 2 minutes. Stir, then microwave on High for another 3 minutes. Stir. Pour the sauce slowly over the pudding batter. Microwave the pudding on Medium-High for 10–12 minutes. Cover and stand for 5 minutes, then serve as suggested.

STEAMED MINCEMEAT PUDDING

Serve this special steamed pudding with Custard (page 43) or Rich Rum Sauce (this page).

60 g/2 oz butter
125 g/4 oz soft brown sugar
2 eggs
250 g/8 oz mincemeat
75 ml/2½ fl oz milk
170 g/5½ oz self-raising flour, sifted
60 g/2 oz nuts, chopped

Cream the butter and sugar well. Stir in the eggs and cream again. Mix in the mincemeat and blend in the milk, flour and nuts. Pour the batter into a greased 2-litre/3½-pint pudding basin (base-lined with waxed paper), cover with pierced cling film and microwave on Medium for 6–8 minutes. The pudding is cooked when a metal skewer inserted into it comes out clean. Stand for 2–3 minutes, invert on to a plate and serve.

RICH RUM SAUCE

250 ml/8 fl oz single cream
12.5 ml/2½ teaspoons cornflour
25 ml/5 teaspoons caster sugar
45 g/1½ oz butter
5 ml/1 teaspoon rum

Combine the cream, cornflour and sugar in a large bowl. Add the butter, Microwave on Medium for 4–5 minutes, stirring after 2 minutes — until thick. Stir in the rum. Serve hot. MAKES 250 ML/8 FL OZ.

GOLDEN STEAMED PUDDING

A family favourite to serve with Custard (page 43) or Brandy Vanilla Sauce (this page).

60 g/2 oz butter
125 g/4 oz soft brown sugar
12.5 ml/2½ teaspoons golden syrup
5 ml/1 teaspoon vanilla extract
125 g/4 oz self-raising flour, sifted
2 eggs
45 ml/3 tablespoons milk
30 ml/2 tablespoons golden syrup

Cream the butter and sugar until light and fluffy. Stir in the syrup, vanilla extract and half of the flour. Beat in the eggs one at a time. Fold in the remaining flour. Stir in the milk to form a soft batter. Spoon the 30 ml/2 tablespoons syrup into the base of a lightly greased pudding basin, swirl it around and pour the batter on top. Cover the bowl with pierced cling film. Microwave on Medium-High for 6–8 minutes — until the pudding shrinks away from the sides of the basin. Stand for 3 minutes, invert on to a serving plate and serve.

BRANDY VANILLA SAUCE

250 ml/8 fl oz milk
60 g/2 oz caster sugar
20 ml/4 teaspoons cornflour
30 g/1 oz butter
10 ml/2 teaspoons brandy
5 ml/1 teaspoon vanilla extract

Mix 200 ml/6½ fl oz of the milk and the sugar in a large jug and microwave on High for 2–3 minutes. Blend the cornflour with the remaining milk. Add the hot milk. Microwave on High for 2 minutes. Stir in the butter, brandy and vanilla. Serve hot. MAKES 250 ML/8 FL OZ.

Steamed Mincemeat Pudding (page 44), Golden Steamed Pudding (page 44) and Custard (page 43).

BAKED ORANGE PUDDING

Serve with whipped cream or Custard (page 43).

ORANGE SYRUP
250 g/8 oz granulated sugar
250 ml/8 fl oz water
30 g/1 oz butter
250 ml/8 fl oz orange juice
5 ml/1 teaspoon grated orange zest

PUDDING
3 eggs
250 g/8 oz caster sugar
185 g/6 oz self-raising flour
pinch of salt
185 ml/6 fl oz milk
30 ml/2 tablespoons oil

grated orange zest to decorate

Combine all the ingredients for the syrup in a bowl and microwave on High for 6 minutes. Keep warm while you make the pudding.

To make the pudding, beat the eggs and caster sugar together until light and creamy. Sift the flour and salt and fold in. Microwave the milk and oil in a jug on High for 40 seconds. Add to the pudding mixture and beat gently. Pour the mixture into a deep, greased bowl. Microwave on High for 6–7 minutes. Stand for 2 minutes, then pour the warm sauce over the pudding, decorate with orange zest and serve.

BAKED APPLE CARAMEL TART

This is sure to become a family favourite!

APPLE TART
75 g/2½ oz butter
250 g/8 oz caster sugar
3 eggs
125 g/4 oz plain flour
7.5 ml/1½ teaspoons baking powder
pinch of salt
60 ml/4 tablespoons milk
410 g/13 oz canned apple pie filling

CARAMEL SAUCE
125 g/4 oz caster sugar
45 g/1½ oz butter
60 ml/4 tablespoons milk
2.5 ml/½ teaspoon caramel extract

5 ml/1 teaspoon ground cinnamon

Cream the butter and caster sugar for the tart together. Add the eggs, one at a time, beating well. Sift the flour, baking powder and salt together and add, alternately with the milk. Pour the mixture into a deep, greased pie dish and top with the apples. Microwave on Medium-High for 14–15 minutes.

Place all the ingredients for the sauce in a deep jug and microwave on High for 2–3 minutes, stirring twice. Pour the sauce over the hot tart, and leave to cool slightly; dust with cinnamon and serve.

COMBINATION OVEN: Cook the tart at 200 °C temperature and medium-low power level for 14–16 minutes (20–25 minutes if your oven alternates convection and microwave energy).

PEACHES WITH STRAWBERRY SAUCE

This dessert makes a refreshingly tasty and colourful end to a meal. If you wish, serve with creamy vanilla ice cream or whipped cream.

STRAWBERRY SAUCE
200 g/6½ oz strawberries, roughly chopped
45 ml/3 tablespoons brandy
45 g/1½ oz caster sugar
15 ml/1 tablespoon Kirsch

4 large peaches, peeled
500 ml/16 fl oz orange juice
200 g/6½ granulated sugar
1 stick cinnamon
1 whole clove
5 ml/1 teaspoon grated orange zest

Place the strawberries in a bowl and pour the brandy over. Leave to soak for 1 hour (you can prepare the peaches while the strawberries are soaking). Stir in the sugar and microwave on High for 4–5 minutes — until the fruit is soft. Stir in the Kirsch, then strain the sauce into a jug for serving cold with the peaches.

Place the peaches in a bowl with water to cover. Mix the orange juice, sugar, cinnamon, clove and orange zest in another bowl and microwave on High for 6–8 minutes — until boiling. Add the peaches. Cover and microwave on Medium-High for 10–12 minutes — until the peaches are slightly soft (cooking time depends on the ripeness of the peaches). Remove the peaches from the syrup and place them in a serving bowl. Microwave the remaining syrup on High for 8–10 minutes to reduce slightly. Remove the whole spices, then pour the syrup over the peaches and leave to cool.

To serve, place a peach in each of four dessert bowls, spoon the syrup over and pour the sauce around.

TROPICAL MOUSSE

440 g/14 oz canned crushed pineapple,
    drained and juice reserved
25 ml/5 teaspoons powdered gelatine
345 g/11 oz pawpaw, peeled and chopped
1 mango, peeled and chopped
155 g/5 oz caster sugar
juice of 1 lemon
250 ml/8 fl oz whipping cream, whipped
3 egg whites
whipped cream, sliced mango and
    pineapple pieces to decorate

Pour 75 ml/2½ fl oz of the reserved juice into a bowl. Sprinkle the gelatine over and allow to expand. Process the pawpaw, mango, pineapple, sugar and lemon juice until smooth. Microwave the gelatine and pineapple juice mixture on High for about 40 seconds — until it just starts to boil. Add to the fruit and mix well. Blend the cream with the fruit mixture. Beat the egg whites until stiff and fold gently into the fruit mixture with a metal spoon. Pour the mousse into a serving bowl and refrigerate for 3–4 hours — until set. Decorate with whipped cream, sliced mango and pineapple pieces.

CREME CARAMEL

A scrumptiously rich dessert.

45 ml/3 tablespoons water
100 g/3½ oz caster sugar
500 ml/16 fl oz milk
4 large eggs, beaten
60 g/2 oz caster sugar
5 ml/1 teaspoon vanilla extract
pinch of salt

Place the water and 100 g/3½ oz caster sugar in a bowl and microwave on High for 6–8 minutes — until golden brown. Do not stir. Coat the insides of six ramekins with the caramel mixture and set aside.

Microwave the milk in a jug on High for 3–4 minutes — until hot but not boiling. Beat the remaining ingredients together lightly. Gradually beat in the hot milk. Strain the mixture and pour it into the ramekins. Place the ramekins, evenly spaced, in a circle on the outer rim of the turntable. Microwave on Medium-Low for 20–25 minutes — until softly set. Stand for 20 minutes to cool, then refrigerate, preferably overnight. Unmould to serve with double cream, if liked.

Peaches with Strawberry Sauce (page 46) and Tropical Mousse (this page).

INDEX
. . . .